PRACTICAL ACTIVITIES
for
PRACTICALLY EVERYTHING

By
CAROLE COOK and JODY CARLISLE

Fearon Teacher Aids
Simon & Schuster Supplementary Education Group

Editor: Carol Williams
Copyeditor: Diane Sovljanski
Illustration and design: Sally Cox

ISBN 0-8224-5576-5

Printed in the United States of America
1. 9 8 7 6 5 4 3 2

TABLE OF CONTENTS

LANGUAGE ARTS (cont.)

MATHEMATICS (cont.)

SPECIAL UNITS

INTRODUCTION

Are you in need of quick and handy activities to teach and motivate your students? *Practical Activities for Practically Everything* offers just that. You will find a variety of ideas that help introduce or reinforce concepts in language arts and mathematics. A special units section is also included to provide seasonal, holiday, and science activities.

Some activities are marked with to indicate that the activity requires a chalkboard or chart and that students will be able to do the activity completely independently. These activities will be especially useful when you divide your class up for reading or math groups. Children can independently work at their desks while you work with a small group. Before children begin the activity, write the necessary sentences or word lists and the "Directions to children" on the chalkboard. For younger children, you might want to write the words or sentences in a format, using ruled paper so that children will understand clearly how to copy the information on their own papers.

Also, write the "Early bird" directions on the chalkboard for students to read and follow if they finish the assigned activity before the work period is over.

Each content area provides reproducible worksheets that can be used for follow-up, sent home with students for homework practice, or used as an indicator of student progress and comprehension of each skill.

Although some activities are designed for independent student work and others are teacher-directed, you can vary the format, depending on the level of your students. You may find it necessary to guide younger students through the steps of a chalkboard activity until they are able to read and follow directions on their own. Older students may be able to do many of the teacher-directed activities with very little assistance. Each activity can also be adapted for use with a small group or a whole class. Tailor each activity to meet the individual needs of your students.

Many of the activities require children to fold their papers to make a certain number of answer boxes before beginning an activity. Display charts in your classroom, using the diagrams below, to show children how to achieve the correct number of boxes. Once they are familiar with the folding process, this preparation step will take less time. Demonstrate the paper-folding steps for younger children until they are able to fold their papers independently. Older children can follow the diagrams and fold their papers themselves.

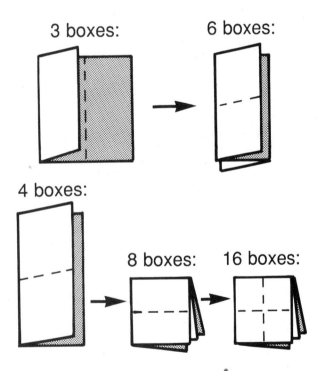

3 boxes: 6 boxes:

4 boxes:

8 boxes: 16 boxes:

LANGUAGE ARTS

HIDDEN PICTURES

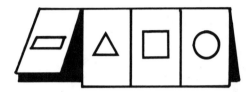

Fold a 12" x 18" piece of tagboard lengthwise. Cut the top flap into four equal sections and tape a geometric shape in each section. Give each child a 9" x 12" piece of construction paper that has been folded lengthwise. Have each child cut the top flap of his or her paper into four equal sections like your sample. (It might be helpful to have the children fold the paper into fourths first so that they have fold lines to cut on.) Children can draw the shapes on their flaps to match the shapes on your tagboard model. Have children find and cut out magazine pictures that match the shapes on the flaps. Children glue one shape under each matching flap.

■

MAKE IT AND PLAY IT

Give each child a 3" x 12" piece of colored construction paper that has been folded into thirds. Have children draw three identical animals—one in each box. Children can color two animals alike and one animal differently. They can trade animal strips and find the animal that is colored differently on each strip. For greater durability, laminate the strips (or cover with clear contact paper) after the children have drawn and colored the animals. Put the strips in an activity center for children to play with independently.

Children can trace around their hands on construction paper and carefully cut out the handprints. Put the children in groups of three or four and ask them to determine whose pair of handprints is biggest, smallest, and whose handprints are about the same size.

GIVE ME A HAND

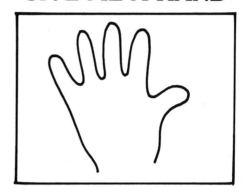

IN THE NEWS

■

Give each child a 9" x 12" piece of newsprint that has been folded into fourths. Draw a model of the paper on the chalkboard and print a letter in each box. Have children copy the letters onto their papers, cut out letters from newspapers or magazines, and glue the letters in the matching boxes on their papers.

LETTER FIND

 Copy the following format on the chalkboard:

A K A A T A
M M O P M M
F F F G H F
R P S R R C
B B D B E B

Directions to Children:

Copy the letters on your paper. Put a circle around the letters in each row that are like the first one.

Early Birds:

Write the letters B and M very large on a piece of art paper. Decorate the M with macaroni and the B with beans.

■

WORD HUNT

 Copy the following format on the chalkboard:

cold sold cold cold
jump jump jump bump
let pet let let
see see me see
boy toy boy boy

Directions to Children:

Copy the words on your paper. Put an X on the word in each row that is different from the first one.

Early Birds:

Using a crayon, draw an outline around one of the words on your paper to make an interesting box shape. Draw around the word two more times, using different colors.

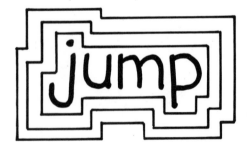

Name: _____

Rabbits, Kites, and Things

Directions:
Color the pictures in each row that are alike.

Name: _____

Letter Hunt

Directions:
Find the hidden letters. Circle them.

Write the word *red* on a 24" x 36" piece of red construction paper. Ask children to cut out pictures from magazines that show something red and to glue the pictures on the red construction paper. Do the same for other color words. Compile the pages to make a class book. Use the book for further classroom discussions about how colors make us feel.

THE BIG BOOK

Make an 8-page booklet (4 1/2" x 6") for each child. Write a color word on each page. Ask children to find as many color words as they can in magazines and glue them in the booklets on the appropriate pages. If no color words can be found, the children can cut apart individual letters to make the color words. Or, they can glue one small picture of that color on each page.

THE LITTLE BOOK

COLOR BOXES

Give each child a 9" x 12" piece of paper that has been folded into fourths. Write a list of color words on the chalkboard. Have each child choose four words and write one word in each box. Ask children to draw and color a picture in each box, using the color of crayon that matches the color word in that box.

■

BALLOON COLLAGE

Cut a balloon shape from construction paper for each child. Use a variety of colors. Have children cut pictures from magazines that match the color of their balloons and glue them on the balloons. Attach a piece of string to each balloon when children are finished. Display the balloons on a colorful bulletin board. Use the bulletin board to review color words.

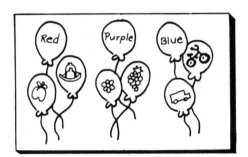

■

COLORS GALORE

 Copy the following format on the chalkboard:

    red red go Red red
    purple is Purple purple
    brown brown see Brown
    orange Orange can orange
    blue two Blue blue

Directions to Children:

Copy the words onto your paper. Underline the color words, using a crayon of that color.

Early Birds:

On the back of your paper, draw a picture of an orange and blue cat. Draw purple whiskers on the cat. Draw a brown dog with a red nose.

Name: _____

Color Concentration

Directions:
Color each balloon, using a crayon the color of the color word. Cut the cards apart and play "Concentration" with a friend. Turn the cards face down on your desk. Take turns turning over two cards at a time to find matching pairs.

red	orange
purple	yellow
blue	brown
green	red
yellow	purple
orange	blue
brown	green

THE REAL THING

Pass out to each child an object that begins with the sound of a letter you are studying. Children can cut out magazine pictures that begin with the same sound and put them into or attach them on the object.

B - small boxes
C - cans
D - doilies
F - folders
G - gold
H - hooks
J - jars
K - paper keys
L - lids (plastic)
M - margarine tubs
N - netting
P - paper
Q - queen
R - rope
S - sandwich
T - paper tubes
V - valentine shapes
W - wire (bread bag fasteners)
Y - yarn
Z - old used zippers

SOCKS

Give each child a sock with four objects in it and a piece of paper. Have children fold their papers to make four boxes. Each child reaches into the sock and takes out one object. The child draws a picture of that object and writes the beginning consonant in one of the boxes on the paper. Repeat with the other three objects in the sock.

Variation:

Children can write the ending sound or the entire word instead of the beginning consonant.

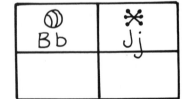

Give each child a turkey body (without feathers) and several paper strips. Have children find as many words that begin with "T" as possible in newspapers or magazines and glue one word on each paper strip. The paper strips can be glued onto the turkey body for feathers. Children color the turkey body and then read the words on their feathers to the class.

TURKEY FEATHERS

PICTURES AND SOUNDS

∎

 Write eight different letters on the chalkboard.

Directions to Children:

Fold your paper into eight boxes. Copy one letter in each box. Draw a picture that begins with each letter in the boxes.

Early Birds:

On the back of your paper, write a big letter that has your favorite sound. Decorate the letter with colors or pictures that begin with that sound.

Dd	Cc
Mm	Nn
Ll	Hh
Bb	Gg

FIND THE WORD!

 Draw a picture of a ring, a sun, a cup, and a pineapple on the chalkboard.

Directions to Children:

Draw one picture on each line of your paper and color the pictures. Find two words in your reading book that begin with the same sound as each picture and write them on the lines.

Early Birds:

On one page in a newspaper, find as many words as you can that begin with one of these sounds. Draw a red box around each word.

Name: _____

At the Zoo

Directions:
Write the beginning sound for each animal in the boxes. Write the sound you think each animal makes in the bubbles.

Clowning Around

Directions:
Color the words that begin like:

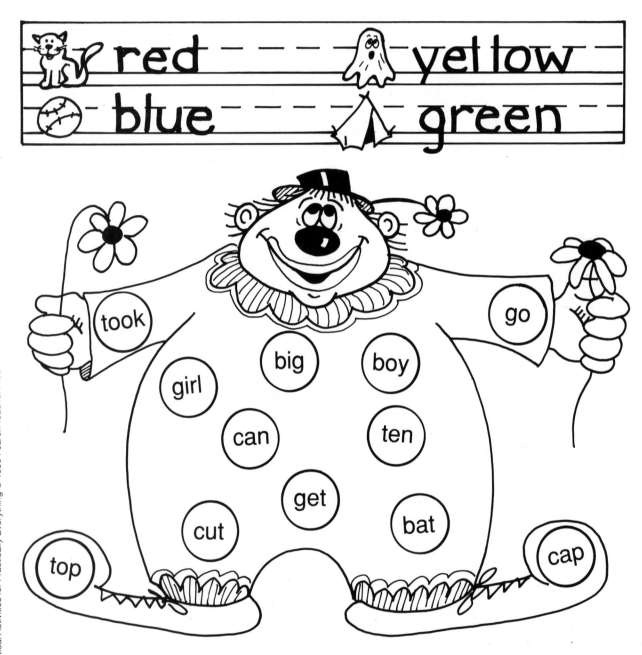

red   yellow

blue   green

took go big boy girl can ten get cut bat top cap

Have each child cut out eight words from magazines or newspapers that end with "M" and nine construction paper circles (provide a pattern for children to trace). Children glue one word on each circle and add face details to the ninth circle. Children can glue their circles together to make worms.

Variation:

Have children make worms, using words with other ending consonants.

WORMY ENDINGS

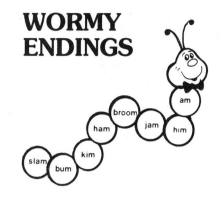

■

Have each child fold an 8 1/2" x 11" sheet of paper in half lengthwise and cut the top flap into thirds. Have children print an ending sound on each flap. Children cut out a magazine picture that ends with each sound and then glue the pictures under the appropriate flaps.

Variation:

Reverse the activity and have children cut out and glue three pictures under the flaps first and then write the ending sounds on top of the flaps.

FLIP UP

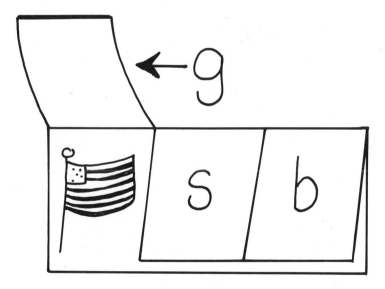

IT'S IN THE BAG

Decorate several lunch bags with bright colors and label each bag with a number. Put several objects with numbered tags attached into each bag. A child can take a bag to his or her desk, remove the objects, and record each object's ending sound on a piece of paper. Have the children number the answers on their papers to correspond with the numbers attached to each object. Ask the children to record the bag number on their papers also.

■

WHEEL OF FORTUNE

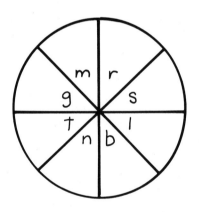

Draw a circle on the chalkboard, divide it into eight sections, and write a letter of the alphabet in each section.

Directions to Children:

Copy the wheel on your paper and write the letters. Cut pictures from magazines or draw a picture for each ending sound.

Early Birds:

For each letter on the wheel, write the name of one of your friends that ends with that letter's sound.

Hint:

You might want to give students some help to divide their circles into eight sections by providing these step-by-step pictures.

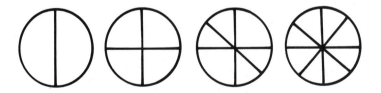

Name: _____

Just Ducky

Directions:
Choose from the list of words to fill in the blanks. Then read the paragraph and complete the picture.

warm	again	duck	water	went
cool	out	pond	sun	

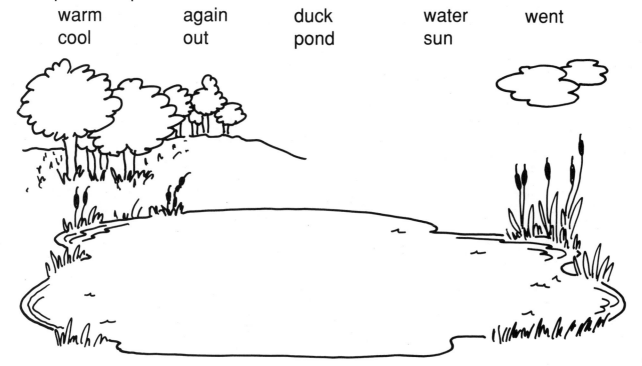

The little _____ went into the _____ .
                   k   d

The _____ was very _____ . "I will get _____ ,"
       r   l   t

said the duck. When the _____ came out, it was _____ .
                               n   m

In _____ the duck _____ .
     t   n

Hint:
The letter underneath each blank is the ending sound for the word that belongs in the blank.

Practical Activities for Practically Everything © 1990 Fearon Teacher Aids

Name: _____

Magic Circus Hat

Directions:
Cut on the dotted line. Cut out the stars with animal pictures on them. Glue each animal onto the star that has the animal's name written on it.

- ✂

Distribute 9" x 12" sheets of newsprint to each of the children and ask them to fold the paper to make eight boxes. Have the children draw a large soup bowl in each box. Give the children each a tablespoon of macaroni alphabet letters to make short-vowel words. Have them glue one word on each soup bowl.

■

 Write the following list of words on the chalkboard:

pen
pan
man
men
beg
bag

Directions to Children:

Write "short a" on the top of one side of your paper. Write "short e" on the top of the other side. Read the list of words to yourself. Listen to the vowel in the middle. Write each word under the correct heading and draw a picture of each word beside it.

Early Birds:

If your name has a short vowel sound in it, write the word "yes," using many different colors of crayons, on the back of your paper. If your name does not have a short vowel sound, write "no" three times, using only your green crayon.

ALPHABET SOUP

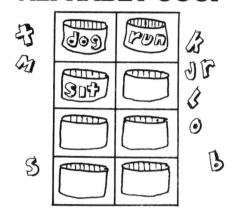

LOOK, LISTEN, AND DO

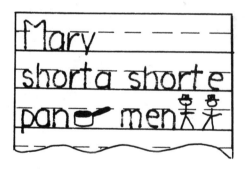

WHAT'S IN THE BAGGIE?

Give each child a small plastic bag containing eight words with short vowels. Children can remove the words, write each one on a sheet of lined paper, and draw an illustration next to each word.

■

RED IS BEST

 Write the following list of words on the chalkboard:

cat	map
net	no
play	me
see	sad
hug	boy
look	dog
milk	the
cake	pig

Directions to Children:

Number your paper to 8. Find eight words in the list that have a short vowel sound and write them on your paper. Draw a picture of each word.

Early Birds:

On the back of your paper, write the names of three friends who have short vowels in their names.

Don't Bug Me!

Directions:
Use your reading book to find a short vowel word to write on each spot on the bug. Color the bug.

Practical Activities for Practically Everything © 1990 Fearon Teacher Aids

Name: _____

Crown Jewels

Directions:
    Color all short ĕ words red.
    Color all short ă words green.
    Color all short ĭ words blue.
    Color all other words white.
    Color the crown yellow.

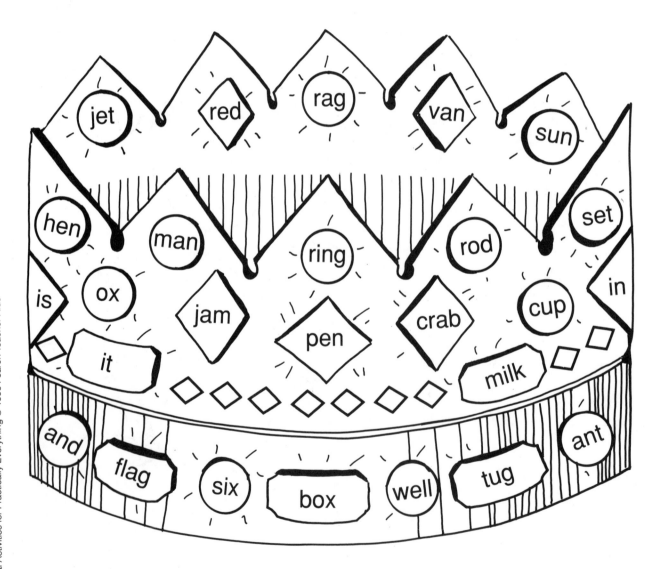

NEAT ANIMALS

Write the following long-vowel animal names on the chalkboard:

beaver	lion
snake	snail
cheetah	seal
ape	bee
sheep	goat
tiger	whale

Have each child make an animal from the list, using construction paper. Display the finished animals on a bulletin board with the animal names under the pictures.

■

MIXED-UP VOWELS

Place slips of paper with a long- or short-vowel word written on each in a mixing bowl. Each child can take ten words from the bowl and write them on a sheet of paper. Have children write "yes" after words that have a long vowel sound and "no" after words that do not. Be sure to remind children to return the words to the bowl when they have finished, so others can use them.

ACTION!

ABC Copy the following list of action words on the chalkboard:

run	hike	sit
jump	climb	ride
walk	jog	swim
cut	dance	tap
sleep	wipe	hop
hug	smile	rake

Directions to Children:

Read the words on the board to yourself. Copy only the action words that have long vowel sounds on your paper.

Early Birds:

On the back of your paper, draw a picture of one of the action words.

■

ANIMAL SNAPSHOTS

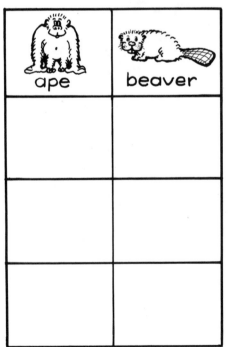

ABC Write the list of animal names on the chalkboard. Provide the students with books that have pictures of animals.

tiger
sheep
goat
cheetah
beaver
lion
ape
snake

Directions to Children:

Fold your paper to make eight boxes. Copy one animal name in each box. Draw a picture of each animal and color it. You may look at some of the animal books in the room if you need help drawing the animals.

Early Birds:

Find a picture of one of these animals in a magazine. Cut it out and glue it on the back of your paper.

ABC Copy the following list of words on the chalkboard:

run	skip
goat	bad
man	pen
is	king
hop	map
bake	ride
go	play
seat	home
pail	flea
sheep	vest

MAKE YOUR MARK

Directions to Children:

Copy the words on your paper. Mark the short vowels with a purple ⌣. Mark the long vowels with an orange —. Cross out the silent vowels with a black ╱.

Early Birds:

On the back of your paper, draw a picture that has four of the long-vowel words in it.

Variation:

Prepare the words on a reproducible page for students to mark.

What's Cooking?

Directions:
Cut on the dotted line. Cut the words apart. Glue the long-vowel words in the mixing bowl.

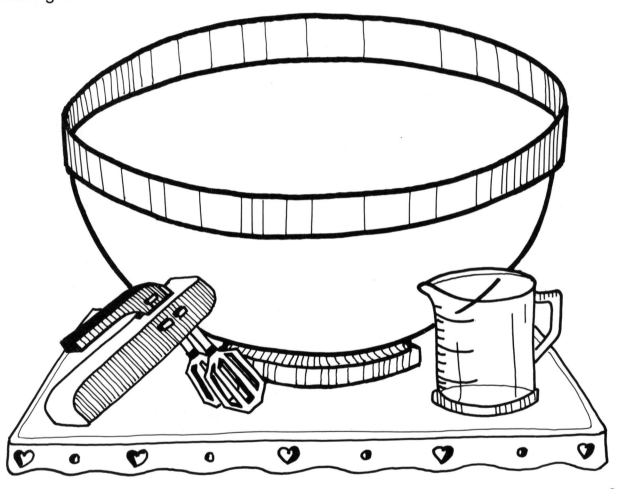

bake	salt	pie	mix	cheese	heat
rise	pan	bowl	cake	stove	hot

Name: _____

Long Dinosaur

Directions:
Circle each long-vowel word below that could be part of a dinosaur picture.
Draw a picture of the words you circled.

1. tree	5. man	9. plane
2. car	6. bee	10. mice
3. rain	7. truck	11. bug
4. train	8. cave	12. snake

ON THE BALL

Have the children each draw and cut out a circle from a piece of 4 1/2" x 6" light-colored construction paper. Then ask them to draw a zigzag line through the circle to divide it into two pieces. Provide a list of compound words. Each child chooses a word and writes half of the word to the left of the zigzag line and the other half of the word to the right of the line on the circle. Have children illustrate the words and then cut their puzzles apart on the zigzag line. Laminate or cover the puzzles with clear contact paper and store them in one large plastic bag.

■

PICK FOUR!

On a green slip of paper, print the first part of a compound word and place it in a basket. On a red slip of paper, print the second part of the compound word and place it in another basket. Do the same with about 15 words and print each of the 15 words twice. Give the children each a piece of paper to fold into fourths. Have them pick four slips of paper from both baskets and try to put the word slips together to make compound words. As words are made, children can copy them in the boxes on their papers and add illustrations. Children can create nonsense words with slips that do not form real compound words. Have students draw a star on their papers beside the nonsense words.

snow ball ⭐⭐ 🏐 snowball ☁	rain house rainhouse ☆

ABC Copy the following two lists of words on the chalkboard:

A	B
light	bow
butter	ball
snow	house
fire	fly
rain	truck

WHAT CAN IT BE?

Directions to Children:

Read the two lists of words. Match each word from list A with a word from list B to make five compound words. Write each word on your paper and draw a picture of it.

Early Birds:

Find pictures in a magazine to illustrate two of the compound words. Glue them on the back of your paper.

■

ABC Copy the following list of compound words on the chalkboard:

raindrop	cupcake
birdhouse	honeybee
mailman	bluebird
eyeball	bookworm
playhouse	grapefruit
salesman	cobweb
goldfish	cornbread

TWO IN ONE

Directions to Children:

Fold your paper to make eight boxes. Choose eight compound words from the list and write one in each box on your paper. Draw an illustration to go with each word.

Early Birds:

On the back of your paper, write the words from the list that are foods. Circle the food you like best.

Name: _____

Where's the Fire?

Directions:
Cut on the dotted line. Cut the words apart. Glue each word next to the picture the compound word tells about.

fire [ ]

fire [ ]

fire [ ]

fire [ ]

fire [ ]

fire [ ]

- ✂

| fly | cracker | truck | wood | place | man |

38 COMPOUND WORDS

Name: _____

Let's Have a Picnic

Directions:
Cut on the dotted line. Cut the pictures apart. Glue each food picture on the word that tells about it.

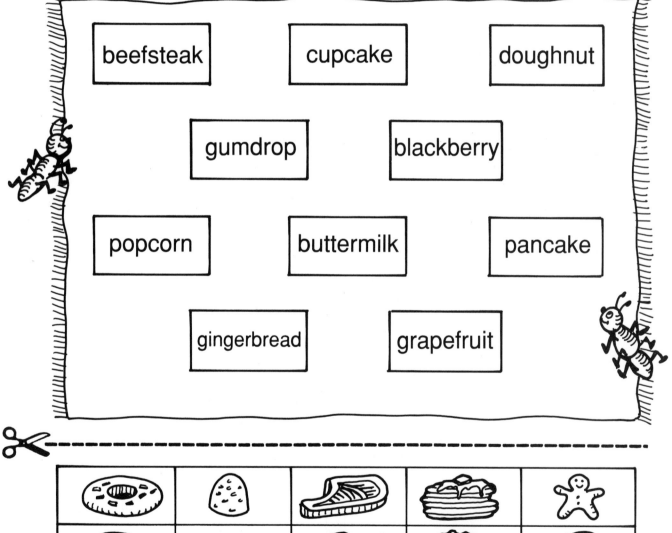

beefsteak	cupcake	doughnut
	gumdrop	blackberry
popcorn	buttermilk	pancake
	gingerbread	grapefruit

✂ -

Practical Activities for Practically Everything © 1990 Fearon Teacher Aids

TAKE YOUR PICK

Decorate a coffee can or oatmeal box and place sentences written on 1" x 8" strips of paper inside. A child can pick a sentence, illustrate it on a large sheet of construction paper, copy the sentence at the bottom of the paper, and underline the rhyming words. Put all the pages together to make a class book of rhymes.

Sentence suggestions:

A pig can have a wig.
The bug is in a jug.
A bear can eat a pear.
The cake fell into the lake.
The frog sat on a log.
The boy likes to run in the sun.
The king wears a huge ring.
She threw a rock at the clock.
A black fox was eating the box.

■

LITTLE BOOKS

Give each child a booklet made by folding four 4 1/2" x 12" pieces of colored construction paper in half and stapling the folded edge. Ask children to number the pages from 1 to 14. Copy the following list of page numbers and words on the chalkboard:

1 book
3 hill
5 wing
7 star
9 toy
11 box
13 pen

Have children copy and illustrate each word on the correct page. Then ask the children to write and illustrate a word that rhymes with each word on the empty page next to it.

Give each child three 3" x 6" pieces of tagboard or other sturdy paper. Have children make a zigzag line in the middle of each piece of tagboard. Ask them to write a word and draw a picture of the word on one side of the line and write the rhyming word and draw a picture of it on the other side of the line. Children can cut the pieces apart on the zigzag lines to make puzzles. Store several puzzles in a plastic bag to use later as a center activity.

PUZZLED

∎

ᴬᴮᴄ Write the following directions on the chalkboard for students to read and follow.

RHYME TIME

Directions to Children:

Fold your paper to make eight boxes and number the boxes from 1 to 8.

In box 1, draw a picture of something that rhymes with "cat."

In box 2, change one letter in the word "wall" to name something you can throw.

In box 3, write a word that rhymes with "lake."

In box 4, write a word that rhymes with "hug" and crawls.

In box 5, draw a picture of a word that rhymes with "hop."

In box 6, write a word that rhymes with "bow" and falls from the sky.

In box 7, change one letter in "mouse" to name a place to live.

In box 8, write a word that rhymes with "pot."

Early Birds:

On the back of your paper, write as many words as you can think of that rhyme with "cat."

Variation:

These directions can also be given orally for students to follow.

CATCH A LITTLE RHYME

bear	pig

ABC Write the following list of words on the chalkboard:

bear
pig
nail
pan
pear
wig
mail
fan

Directions to Children:

Fold your paper to make eight boxes. Write one word in each box and draw a picture of something that rhymes with each word.

Early Birds:

Cut out pictures from magazines of words that rhyme. Glue them on the back of your paper.

■

FAT CAT AND RAT

ABC Copy the following sentences on the chalkboard:

The fat cat sat on a mat.
The rat gave the cat a pat with a bat.

Directions to Children:

Copy each sentence. Draw an orange line under each word with "at" in it.

Early Birds:

Draw a picture of these two funny sentences on the back of your paper.

It's a Rhyme

Directions:
Cut on the dotted line. Cut the words apart and glue them in the column under the picture that rhymes.

bug	cat	cake	star

✂ -

car	make	Pat	mug
jug	bake	far	sat
take	mat	dug	jar
bar	rug	rat	lake

Name: _____

Henny Penny

Directions:
Circle the words that rhyme with "hen." Find the number word and draw that many chicks under the hen. Color the picture.

Give each child a copy of an ice-cream cone scoop pattern and write the pairs of words on the chalkboard. Have each child trace and cut out five scoops from colored construction paper and write a word pair on each scoop. Children can glue the scoops on a sheet of paper and draw an ice-cream cone underneath each scoop. Children can write the contractions that can be made from each pair of words on the cones.

do not
I will
he would
could not
they are

SCOOPS GALORE

CARDS, CARDS EVERYWHERE

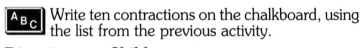

Provide a bucket of cards with the following contractions written on them. (Write each contraction on more than one card.)

can't	isn't	we've
don't	wouldn't	he's
didn't	I'll	we're
couldn't	won't	they'll
hasn't	she's	aren't
haven't	they're	hadn't

Each child can choose three cards from the tub, take them back to his or her desk, and write a sentence containing the contraction and a sentence containing the two words that the contraction represents.

■

GO TOGETHERS

ABC Write ten contractions on the chalkboard, using the list from the previous activity.

Directions to Children:

Copy each contraction and write the two words that make up the contraction beside it.

Early Birds:

Cut out two contractions from a newspaper or magazine and glue them on the back of your paper.

Provide children with a mitten pattern to trace and cut out two pairs of mittens. Have children attach the pairs with yarn. Write the following lists on the chalkboard:

A	B
you'd	we have
that's	can not
they'll	that is
won't	you would
wasn't	they will
can't	was not
we've	will not

Each child can choose a contraction from list A to write on one mitten and write the two words from list B that make up the contraction on the other mitten. Repeat with other pairs of mittens.

∎

Have students fold a sheet of plain paper to make eight boxes and unfold the paper until it is folded in half lengthwise. Instruct students to cut through only the top flap on the fold lines to make four flaps. Have students write one pair of words from the following list on each flap:

had not
she will
is not
does not
they are
will not
could not
he is
are not
should not
we are

Students can decorate the flaps to make the paper look like a four-story house. Have them open each flap and write the contraction underneath for the word pair.

PERFECT PAIRS

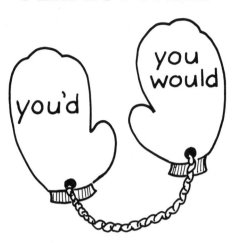

HOUSE OF CONTRACTIONS

Name: _____

Bees and Flowers

Directions:
Cut on the dotted line. Cut out the bees and match them to the correct flowers. Glue in place.

Name: _____

Piggyback Trucks

Directions:
Cut on the dotted line. Cut out the piggyback trailers and connect them to the correct trucks. Glue in place.

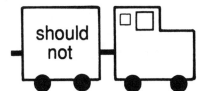

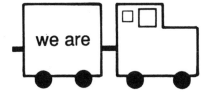

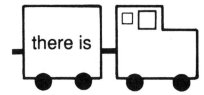

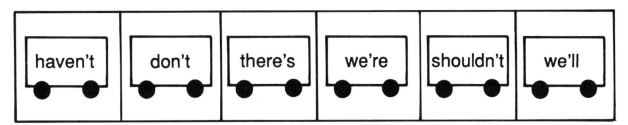

Practical Activities for Practically Everything © 1990 Fearon Teacher Aids

CONTRACTIONS 49

MACARONI FUN

Give the children each ten pieces of alphabet macaroni. Have them place the letters that they receive in alphabetical order. (Remind the children that the letters still need to appear in their proper order even if some letters are missing.) Have the children glue the letters in order vertically on their papers and draw a picture that begins with each letter.

■

ENVELOPE ALPHABETIZING

Give the children each an envelope containing familiar words from their spelling or reading book. Have them place the words in alphabetical order and then glue the words on a piece of paper, leaving a large space between each word. The children can find words in a magazine or newspaper that begin with letters of the alphabet that come between the words and glue them in place.

■

TOP HAT

Give each student five small slips of paper. Have the children neatly write the name of someone in the classroom on each slip. Ask the children to place the names in a top hat. When all the names are in the hat, each student draws out five slips, takes them to his or her desk, and writes the names in alphabetical order on a piece of paper. Students can pass their papers to a partner to check for accuracy.

Variation:

Have students use names of animals, food, cars, states, cities, flowers, or anything else that complements a current unit of study.

ABC WORD FUN

ABC Copy the blanks and list of words on the chalkboard.

1. _____ dog _____
2. _____ winter_____
3. _____ morning _____
4. _____ rain_____
5. _____ jog _____

Directions to Children:

Copy the list of words and blank lines on your paper. Write a word in the first blank that would come before the given word in ABC order. Write a word in the second blank that would come after the given word.

Early Birds:

Write the names of five of your favorite animals in ABC order on the back of your paper.

■

SENTENCE ABC'S

ABC Copy the following mixed-up sentences on the chalkboard:

1. boy earthworms can a dig.
2. kitten overalls Joy's likes my new.
3. peanuts a gave boy us to.
4. pizza wonderful green taste does?
5. waddle duck likes a to.

Directions to Children:

Put the words in each sentence in ABC order as you copy them on your paper. Each sentence should make sense! Remember to begin the first word of the sentence with a capital letter.

Early Birds:

Think of a sentence of your own that is in ABC order. Write it on the back of your paper.

Three-Ring Circus

Directions:
Cut on the dotted line. Cut out the animals and put them in the correct circus ring. The animal's name begins with a letter of the alphabet that would fit between the letter pairs listed beside each circus ring.

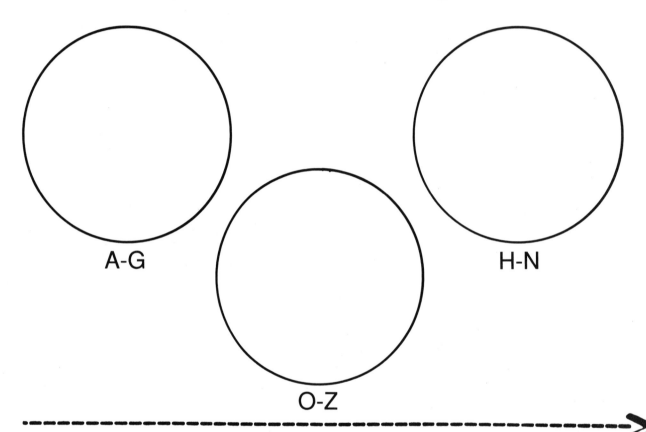

A-G

H-N

O-Z

✂ -

Name: _____

Shop Around

Think about the name of each food item in the bag and the letter of the alphabet it begins with.

1. Color the food that begins with the letter that comes first in the alphabet red.
2. Color the next item yellow.
3. Color the next item green.
4. Color the next item purple.
5. Color the next item white.
6. Color the next item orange.
7. Color the next item red and brown.
8. Color the next item brown.

RIGHT HAND, LEFT HAND

Give each child a 9" x 12" sheet of colored construction paper to trace and cut out one hand. On one side of the hand, have children write something that makes them happy on each finger. On the opposite side of the hand, have them write something that makes them sad on each finger.

Variation:

Try other antonym pairs, such as big/little, clean/dirty, or hot/cold.

■

BIG AND LITTLE

Give each child a large piece of paper and a small piece of paper. Have children write the word "Big" on the large piece and "Little" on the smaller piece. Children cut out pictures from magazines of things that are "big," such as buildings, cars, and trucks, to glue on the large piece of paper and "little" things, such as bugs and eyes, to glue on the small piece.

Variation:

Have children label their pieces of paper with other antonym pairs, such as hot/cold, fat/skinny, old/new, or clean/dirty.

Write the following list of words on the chalkboard:

rich	up
old	hard
laugh	grandma
clean	in
day	ugly
cold	high

UP AND DOWN

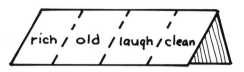

Ask the children each to fold a 9" x 12" piece of paper to make eight boxes and unfold it, leaving it folded in half lengthwise. Have children cut on the fold lines of the top flap only to make four small flaps. The children choose four words from the list and print one on each flap. Then children can lift up each flap and write the antonym underneath. Illustrations can be added.

■

ABC Write the following two lists of words on the chalkboard:

PICTURE PERFECT

A	B
boy	night
day	cold
slim	fat
up	girl
hot	down

Directions to Children:

Fold your paper in half and unfold it. Write the words from list A on the left side of your paper. Write the words in list B on the right side of your paper. Draw a picture for each word and color it. Then draw a line from each word on the left side of the paper to its opposite on the right side.

Early Birds:

On the back of your paper, draw a picture of a slim boy going up a hill on a hot day.

MIX AND MATCH

 Write the following two lists of words on the chalkboard:

A	B
lead	remember
morning	pull
forget	wrong
right	soft
hard	night
push	follow

Directions to Children:

Fold your paper in half and then unfold it. Write the words from list A on the left side of your paper. Write the words from list B on the right side of your paper. Use different colors of crayons to draw lines between the pairs of opposites.

Early Birds:

On the back of your paper, make a list of three things you usually do in the morning and three things you usually do at night.

MIXED-UP OPPOSITES

 Write the following scrambled words on the chalkboard:

og	ptos
ads	yapph
gib	tiltle
pu	ndwo

Directions to Children:

Fold your paper to make eight boxes. Unscramble the words and write one in each box. Draw a picture to go with each word.

Early Birds:

Think of two colors that are opposites. Draw a bird on art paper and color it, using those two colors. Cut out the bird. What is the name of the bird you drew? Does it live where the weather is cold or hot?

Name: _____

Double Dip

Directions:
Cut on the dotted line. Cut out the ice-cream scoops. Some words have two opposites. Glue two ice-cream scoops on each cone to match the antonyms.

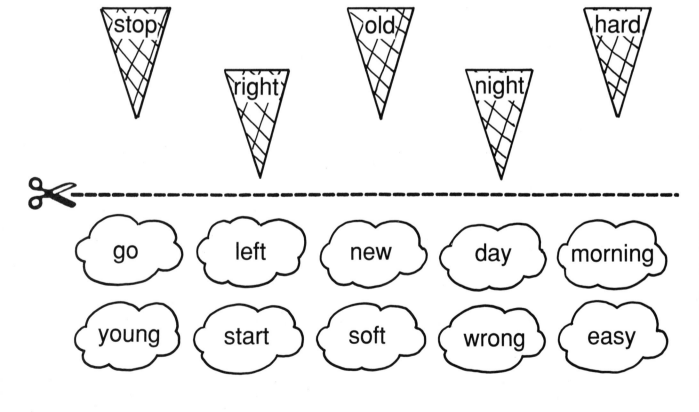

Practical Activities for Practically Everything © 1990 Fearon Teacher Aids

Mystery Word

Directions:
Read each word and write its opposite in the boxes. When you finish, you will see a mystery word that begins in box number 1 and goes down.

Across
1. you
2. close
3. remember
4. over
5. out
6. begin
7. take

The mystery word is _____ .

SENTENCE HUNT

Discuss the three types of sentences (question, statement, exclamatory) with the children. Give each child one page from the newspaper and have children locate one type of each sentence. Children can cut the sentences out and glue them on paper.

Who is that new rock star?

Look at that horse run!

Today is Tuesday.

■

A NAME FOR EVERYTHING

Remind children that all proper nouns must be capitalized. Have each child find three proper nouns in a newspaper and cut them out. Have children write a sentence on paper that uses each name and glue the names in the proper place in each sentence. Remind students to use proper punctuation in the sentences.

I live in the state of Virginia.

■

SENTENCE EXCHANGE

Give each child a strip of adding machine tape to write a sentence without punctuation or capital letters. Have children exchange sentence strips with partners and add punctuation and capital letters where needed. Partners can exchange again to check each other's work.

can you play with samuel

Can you play with Samuel?

LETTER WRITING

 Write the following letter on the chalkboard:

Dear John

I am having a birthday party on Tuesday
Do you think you will be able to come
I sure hope so

Your friend

Bill

Directions to Children:

Copy the letter on your paper and add the correct punctuation marks.

Early Birds:

Design a birthday card for one of your friends.

■

WHAT NEEDS A CAPITAL LETTER?

 Write the following list of words on the chalkboard:

john
virginia
wednesday
friend
lucy
february
walt disney
mickey mouse
san francisco
ball

Directions to Children:

Copy the list of words on your paper. Put a capital letter where needed.

Early Birds:

Cut out three words from the newspaper that should always begin with a capital letter. Glue them on the back of your paper.

Name: _____

Silly Billy Goes for a Walk

Directions:
Find the words that need a capital letter and circle them with a red crayon. Add the missing punctuation marks.

One day Silly Billy went for a walk he came to some blue water. there was a bridge over the water. billy looked into the blue water. "Oh, my!" he said. "A boy has fallen into the water he has red hair just like me he has a brown and orange coat just like me he has blue pants just like me.

A bluebird laughed and laughed "Silly Billy," said the bluebird who do you think you are looking at

Draw a picture of Silly Billy in the space below. Color your picture, using the colors in the story.

Name: _____

Choose Your Banner

Directions:
Circle the correct punctuation mark for each sentence.

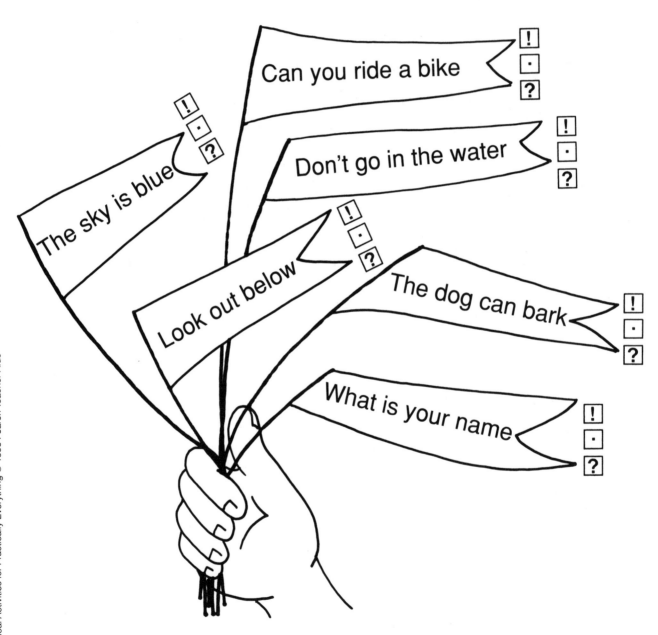

ABBREVIATION HUNT

Give children magazines and newspapers and have them find as many abbreviations as they can and glue them on paper. After each abbreviation, have the children write what the abbreviation stands for.

| Dr. | doctor |
| St. | street |

■

SORTING FUN

Write abbreviations for the days of the week, months of the year, states of the United States, and titles on 3" x 5" cards. Label four baskets with the same categories. Children can sort the cards into the correct baskets.

Months of the Year

Days of the Week

States

Titles

MONTH BY MONTH

ABC Write the following two lists side by side on the chalkboard:

A	B
Feb.	January
Sept.	February
Dec.	August
Aug.	December
Nov.	October
Oct.	September
Jan.	November

Directions to Children:

Copy the abbreviations in list A on your paper. Write each abbreviation's match in list B next to it.

Early Birds:

Pick your favorite month. On the back of your paper, write three things you like about that month. Draw a picture, too.

Variation:

Do the same activity with other lists of abbreviations, such as states or days of the week.

Write the days of the week on the chalkboard.

DAY BY DAY

Tuesday
Wednesday
Sunday
Thursday
Monday
Saturday
Friday

Mary	— —	— —
Tuesday	Tues. —	Mon. —
Wednesday	Wed. —	Tues.
Sunday	Sun. —	Wed.
Thursday	Thurs —	Thurs.
Monday	Mon. —	Fri. —
Saturd	S	at

Directions to Children:

Fold your paper into thirds. Copy each day of the week in the first column. Write the abbreviation for each day in the second column. In the third column, write the abbreviations in order from the first day of the week to the last.

Early Birds:

On the back of your paper, write a paragraph about your favorite day of the week. Or, draw a picture to show your favorite activity to do on that day.

Name: _____

Matchup

Directions:
Cut on the dotted line. Cut out each abbreviation and glue it next to the correct picture.

| Rd. | Dr. | U.S.A. | Oct. | Mtn. | Fla. |

Name: _____

The Long and Short of It

Directions:
Write the abbreviations under the words with boxes. Make a green line on the map to show Mister Smith's path.

On Sunday Mister Smith went to Green Mountain,
[ ] [ ] [ ]

North Carolina, by way of Old Mill Road. He passed
[ ] [ ]

Doctor Sneed at the corner of Maple Avenue and Oak
[ ] [ ]

Street.
[ ]

Green Mountain

doctor

Mr. Smith's house

Maple Avenue

Oak Street

Old Mill

Old Mill Road

Practical Activities for Practically Everything © 1990 Fearon Teacher Aids

COMIC RELIEF

Have the children bring from home a favorite newspaper comic strip. Mount the strips on colored construction paper, number the backs of the frames, and laminate or cover them with clear contact paper. Cut the comic strips apart. Place the frames from each strip in a plastic bag or envelope labeled with the comic strip's name. Children can take the strips to their desks and try to put the frames in the correct order. They can check their work by looking at the numbers on the backs of the frames.

■

THE GINGERBREAD MAN

After reading "The Gingerbread Man" to the children, have children make their own story booklets by folding two pieces of paper in half and stapling the left side. Children can write "The Gingerbread Man" on the front page and a sentence about the story on each of the other pages. Encourage children to write two sentences about the beginning of the story, two about the middle, and two about the end so that their booklets will tell the story in sequence. Children can add illustrations.

Variation:

Use other stories, such as "Three Billy Goats Gruff," "Hansel and Gretel," "The Ugly Duckling," or "Jack and the Beanstalk."

Have each child fold a piece of paper into thirds and think about the steps to make a peanut butter and jelly sandwich. Provide bread cut into quarters, a jar of peanut butter, a jar of jelly, and a butter knife in each jar. Children can make small sandwiches and return to their desks to draw three pictures and write three sentences outlining the steps to make a peanut butter and jelly sandwich. Children can eat their sandwiches when they have finished!

PEANUT BUTTER AND JELLY

■

A B C Copy the following list of numbers on the chalkboard:

12, 52, 1, 9, 26, 63, 47, 38, 100, 88, 18, 73, 94, 14, 32, 6

NUMBER SEQUENCE

Directions to Children:

Fold your paper to make 16 boxes and unfold it. Write one number in each box in the proper order, beginning with 1 and ending with the largest number.

Early Birds:

Write your favorite number between 1 and 20 in the middle of a piece of paper. Draw a set of your favorite toys to match your favorite number.

READY, SET, GO!

 Copy the following sentences on the chalkboard:

1. I wash my face and brush my teeth.
2. I eat breakfast.
3. I get dressed and tie my shoes.
4. I ride the bus to school.
5. I pick up my lunch and books before I leave for school.
6. The alarm wakes me up every morning.

Directions to Children:

Read all six sentences to yourself. Copy the sentences on your paper in the correct order.

Early Birds:

Fold a sheet of paper to make six boxes. Draw a picture of each sentence in the boxes.

■

DOG WASHING

 Directions to Children:

Pretend you have a pet dog. Give your dog a name. Write five sentences about the steps you take when you give your dog a bath. Be sure your sentences are in order. Draw a picture of your dog and write his or her name below the picture.

Early Birds:

On the back of your paper, draw three pictures to show how to brush your teeth.

Name: _____

Building a Snowman

Directions:
Write a number in each small box to correctly order the six steps to build a snowman.

Practical Activities for Practically Everything © 1990 Fearon Teacher Aids

Name: _____

Old Mr. Jack-o'-Lantern

Directions:
Draw a picture to match each sentence. Number the sentences in the correct order.

_____ Then I carved the face of my jack-o'-lantern.

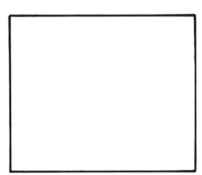

_____ I found my pumpkin in a pumpkin patch.

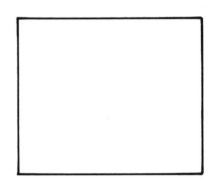

_____ I put a candle inside of my jack-o'-lantern.

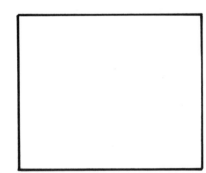

_____ I cut a hole in the top of my pumpkin and took out the seeds.

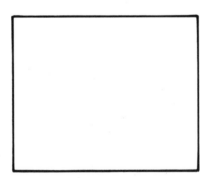

_____ I planted the seeds from my jack-o'-lantern for the next year.

_____ I drew a face on my pumpkin.

MATHEMATICS

BIG FOOT

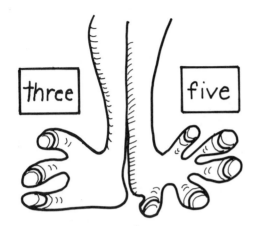

Give each child two pieces of paper with a number word (between one and twenty) written on them. Have the children each draw a pair of monster feet on a piece of construction paper and draw the number of toes on each foot to correspond with the two number words they were given. They can then glue the matching number word beside the appropriate foot.

FUNNY BONES

Directions to Children:

Draw your own funny character with these body parts:

1. two heads
2. four eyes
3. one nose
4. six arms
5. three legs
6. ten fingers on each hand
7. five toes on each foot
8. an unusual body shape

When you complete your drawing, color it!

Early Birds:

Count the number of books that you have inside your desk. Write the number word on your paper beside your name.

Write the following number words on the chalkboard:

three
five
ten
six
eight
two
seven
nine

Directions to Children:

Write each number word on your paper. Glue the correct number of beans beside each number word.

Early Birds:

Count all the beans that you have glued on your paper. On the back of your paper, write the total number of beans.

■

Prepare a large circus train on a bulletin board or classroom wall and label each car with a number word. Give each child a number word written on a slip of paper. Children can draw, color, and cut out as many circus animals as their slips of paper indicate. Children can help display the animals on the bulletin board by putting the correct number of animals in each train car.

BEANS, BEANS EVERYWHERE

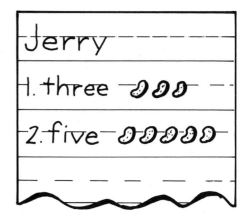

CIRCUS TRAIN

NUMBER MATCHUP

Write the number words from eleven to twenty and the numerals from 11 to 20 on 3" x 5" cards. Children can play concentration with a partner, using the set of 20 cards. The game begins with all cards turned face down. The first player turns over two cards to try to match the number word with the numeral. If a match is made, the player keeps the two cards. If no match is made, the cards are turned back over and the next player tries to make a match.

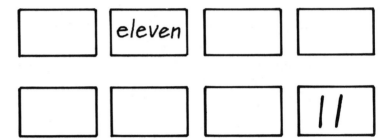

Name: _____

Blowing Bubbles

Directions:
Color the number words between: 1 and 4 orange
                                 5 and 8 green
                                 9 and 13 blue
                                 14 and 16 yellow
                                 17 and 20 red

Practical Activities for Practically Everything © 1990 Fearon Teacher Aids

Name: _____

Off to the Races

Directions:
Cut on the dotted line. Cut out the number words and glue them inside the car with the matching numeral.

twelve	three	thirteen	seventeen	fifteen
six	four	two	nine	eighteen

Have children fold their papers in half and unfold them. Give each child a few popcorn kernels to glue onto one side of the paper. Have children glue the same amount of popped corn on the other side of the paper. Children can write the numeral below each set.

POP UP

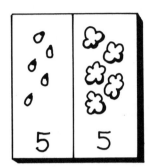

■

Have each child trace one hand with fingers spread on a 9" x 12" piece of paper. Tell each child a number between two and five to write in the corner of the paper. The children draw this number of rings on each of the fingers. After children have drawn the rings, have them write the total number of rings on the page.

HAND JIVE

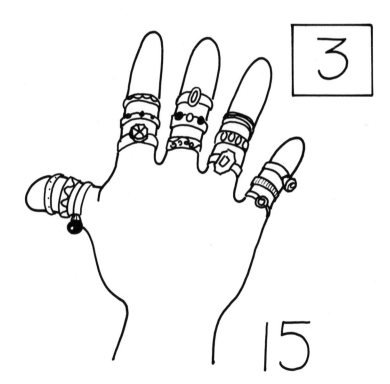

CEREAL COUNT

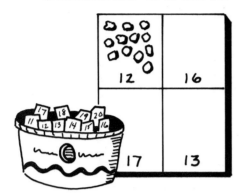

Write the numbers from 11 to 20 on squares of paper (make several sets) and place them in a large plastic margarine tub. Have each child fold a sheet of paper to make four boxes. Each child can draw four slips of paper from the tub and write one number in each box on the paper. Provide small cereal pieces for children to glue on their papers to match the numbers written in the boxes. Eating a few pieces of cereal is part of the fun, too!

■

YOU CAN SEE IT!

ABC **Directions to Children:**

Fold your paper to make six boxes. Draw a picture of something in the room in each box. Count how many objects there are in the classroom to match each picture and write that number next to the picture.

Early Birds:

On the back of your paper, write the numbers from 10 to 20 and circle your favorite number.

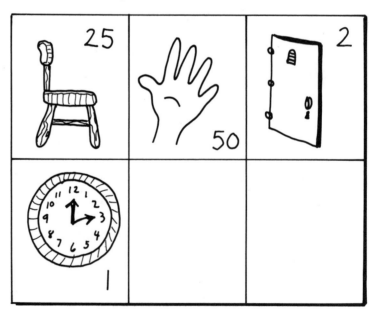

Name: _____

Something Fishy

How many fish have spots? _____

How many fish are swimming to the right? _____

How many fish have stripes? _____

How many fish have big eyes? _____

Practical Activities for Practically Everything © 1990 Fearon Teacher Aids

COUNTING **81**

Name: _____

Red Shirts

Directions:
Each day count the number of people in the classroom who are wearing red (or mostly red) shirts. Color a red square for each shirt in the column for the correct day of the week.

	Mon.	Tues.	Wed.	Thurs.	Fri.
10					
9					
8					
7					
6					
5					
4					
3					
2					
1					

Have each child cut out ten numbers between one and five from the newspaper. Children can make addition problems by gluing the numbers on their papers and writing a plus sign between pairs of numbers. Have children compute the sums and then illustrate the addition facts.

NUMBER GAME

Give each child six 3" x 5" cards. Have children write all of the two number addition combinations that have the sum of five on the front of the cards and write the sum on the backs. Children can take the cards home for flashcard practice.

LEARN THOSE FACTS

Variation:
Make addition facts for other sums below ten.

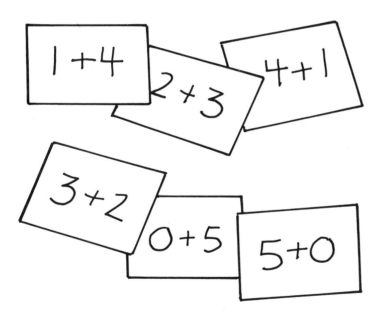

EGG-CITING

Write number word sentences on small strips of paper. Put a sentence strip in each colorful plastic egg and put the eggs in a basket. Each child can choose an egg and copy the number word sentence on paper, using pictures and numbers instead of words. Remind students to return the eggs to the basket when finished, so others can use them.

MY NUMBER STORIES

 Write the numbers from zero to ten on the board.

Directions to Children:

Write five number sentences, using any of these numbers. Be sure to write the answers, too!

Early Birds:

Cut out pictures from a magazine to make a picture story problem on the back of your paper. Write the addition fact and sum for the pictures.

A B C Write the following number sentences on the chalkboard:

1. Two bananas and seven grapes.
2. Five cups and two plates.
3. Three boys and seven girls.
4. Six airplanes and three jets.
5. One red ball and four white balls.

Directions to Children:

Write the sentences, replacing the number words with numbers, and write the sum for each fact.

Early Birds:

Write three math facts on the back of your paper. Glue cereal pieces beside each number to show the correct amount.

■

A B C Copy the following addition problems on the chalkboard:

$3 + 4 + 2 =$
$6 + 0 + 4 =$
$1 + 5 + 1 =$
$3 + 3 + 3 =$
$2 + 7 + 1 =$
$8 + 1 + 0 =$
$0 + 0 + 7 =$
$9 + 1 + 0 =$

Directions to Children:

Fold your paper to make eight boxes. Write one problem in each box, add the numbers, and write the sums.

Early Birds:

On the back of your paper, use a stamp and stamp pad to illustrate two of the number problems.

Name: _____

Monster Math

Directions:
Solve the math problems below. Cut out the toes that have the sum of 8. Glue the toes at the bottom of a large piece of paper. Draw a monster named "Big 8" to go with the toes.

Name: _____

Flying High

Directions:
Cut on the dotted line. Cut out the wings and glue each one to the airplane with the addition problem that matches the sum.

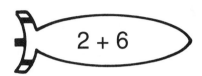

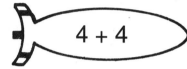

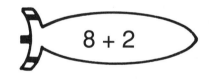

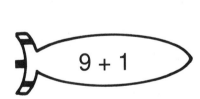

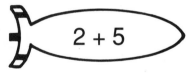

✂ -

 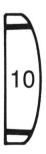  

10   10   8   8   7   9

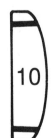

SPILL THE BEANS

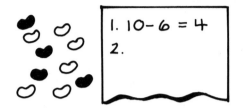

Spread a package of lima beans out on newspaper and spray paint one side of the beans. Let them dry and then divide the beans into sets of ten. Put the sets in plastic bags, and give each child a set of ten beans. Children "spill" the beans on their desks, count the number of beans that land plain side up, and subtract that number from ten. The number of beans that land paint side up provides the answer to the math problem. Have children record the problems and answers on paper.

■

PERFECT PUZZLES

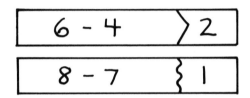

Give each child ten 3" x 9" pieces of paper. Ask children to write a subtraction problem on each piece of paper. Show children how to cut the answers off the end with a zigzag or wavy line to make puzzles. Children can exchange puzzles with partners and try to put them together. Add some excitement by challenging students to solve the puzzles in a certain amount of time.

■

NUMBER PICTURES

Have each child fold three paper strips in thirds. Have children draw pictures on each strip to illustrate the following three word problems written on the chalkboard:

1. Seven kites were flying in the air. Two became stuck in the trees. How many were still flying in the air?
2. Nine ladybugs were on one flower. Four flew away. How many ladybugs were left?
3. Six cans of different-colored paint were on the table. Two cans tipped over. How many cans were left?

On the back of each paper strip, have children write a number sentence that matches the pictures they drew on the front.

ABC **Directions to Children:**

Fold your paper to make four boxes and number the boxes from 1 to 4. Take a bag with 10 M & M's in it.

1. In box number 1, draw how many M & M's you have if you eat none. Write the number sentence.
2. In box number 2, draw how many M & M's you have if you eat 3. Write the number sentence.
3. In box number 3, draw how many M & M's you have if you eat 4. Write the number sentence.
4. In box number 4, draw how many M & M's you have if you eat 3. Write the number sentence.

Early Birds:

On the back of your paper, draw ten of your favorite foods. Show how many would be left if you ate two of them.

ABC Write the following number sentences on the chalkboard:

4 - 3 = ☐
6 - 2 = ☐
5 - 1 = ☐
8 - 2 = ☐
9 - 8 = ☐

Directions to Children:

Copy the number sentences on your paper. Write the answer in each box and draw a picture to show what the number sentence means.

Early Birds:

Draw a rainbow with 8 colors on the back of your paper. Cross out the four colors you like the least. Which four colors do you like best?

M & M FUN

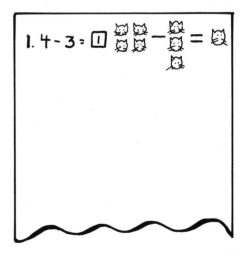

1. 10 - 0 = 10   2. 10 - 3 = 7

3.   4.

PICTURE THAT!

1. 4 - 3 = ☐

Name: _____

Blast Off!

Directions:

Cut on the dotted line. Cut out the number problems and glue them on the correct launching pad.

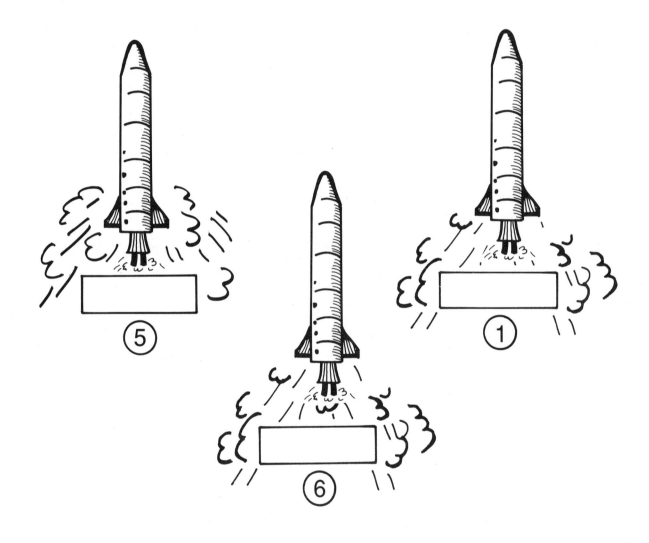

⑤

⑥

①

- ✂

| 9 - 3 | | 8 - 3 | | 6 - 5 |

Name: _____

Red, White, and Blue

Directions:

Answer the problems. Color each section that has an answer of 5 red. Color each section that has an answer of 3 blue.

Cut out the circle and cut a slit on the dotted line. Overlap and glue the section with the answer of 2 on the section without a math problem to make an umbrella. Attach a pipe cleaner for a handle.

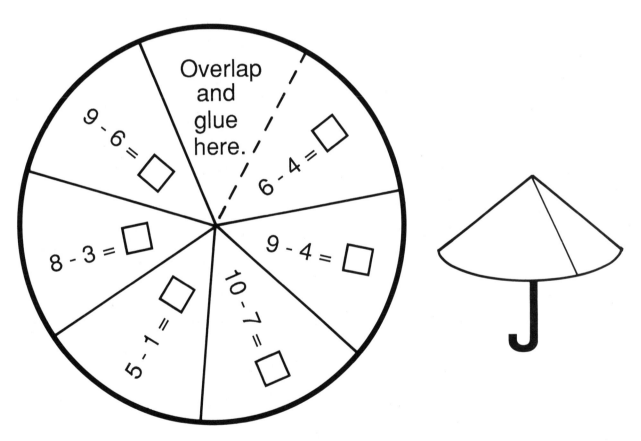

Practical Activities for Practically Everything © 1990 Fearon Teacher Aids

CLOCK WORK

Give each child a paper plate, a brass fastener, and a half sheet of black construction paper. Have each child cut out the numbers 1 to 12 from a newspaper and glue them on the paper plate to make the clock face. Each child can cut an hour and minute hand from the black paper, using the pattern below. The hands can be fastened on the clock face with the brass fastener. When the children have finished constructing their clocks, call out a time and have the students position the hands on their clocks to represent that time.

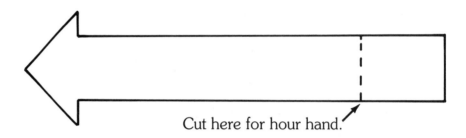

Cut here for hour hand.

WHAT TIME?

Write the following questions on the chalkboard:

What time do you get up each morning?
What time do you go to school?
What time do you come home from school?
What time do you go to bed each night?

Directions to Children:

Fold a sheet of paper to make four boxes and number the boxes from 1 to 4. Draw a clock in each box to provide the answer to each of the four questions.

Early Birds:

On the back of your paper, draw a clock that shows your favorite time of day and explain why that is your favorite time.

Variation:

Ask children other questions such as When do you watch TV? or What time do you eat dinner?

Have students work in pairs, using the clocks they made in the previous activity. Write the following times on the chalkboard and have students practice moving the clock hands. Their partners can check their work.

3:30	1:15	7:10	5:30
12:00	6:45	11:35	8:05
9:00	4:00		

■

ABC Copy the following times on the chalkboard:

10:50	6:10	8:00
4:20	12:40	2:30

Directions to Children:

Fold your paper to make six boxes. Draw a clock in each box. Draw the hands on the clocks to show the correct times. Write the time below each clock.

Early Birds:

On the back of your paper, draw a clock to show your favorite time of day.

■

ABC Draw the clock on the chalkboard.

Directions to Children:

Fold your paper to make four boxes. Using a quarter or a cap from a bottle, trace a small circle in each box. Look at the clock face drawn on the chalkboard and notice what time it says. Make a clock face on your paper that is:

    one hour earlier
    two hours later
    thirty minutes later
    fifteen minutes earlier

Early Birds:

On the back of your paper, draw a clock that is ten hours later than the clock on the chalkboard.

IT'S ABOUT TIME!

TIME FOR A BREAK

ONE MORE TIME!

Name: _____

Cuckoo! Cuckoo!

Directions:

Cut on the dotted line. Cut out the cuckoo birds and glue them on the clocks that show time to the hour or half hour.

Name: _____

Follow the Path

Directions:
Follow the path as you color the clocks. Be careful not to take the wrong path.

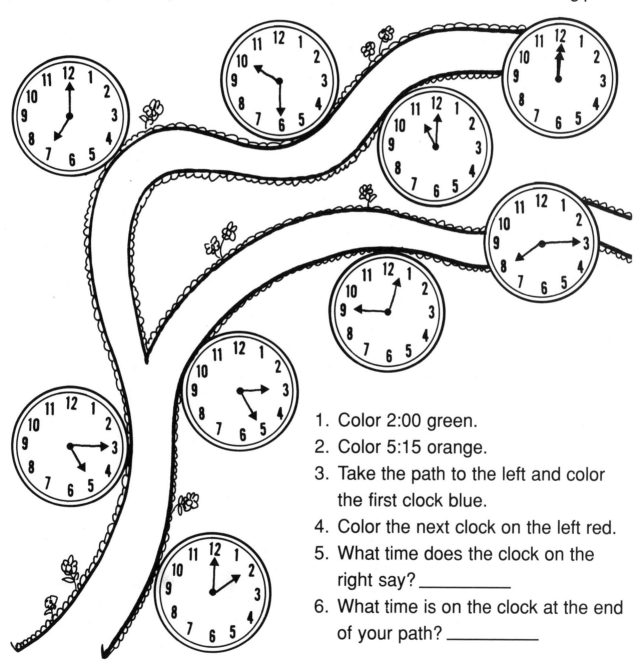

1. Color 2:00 green.
2. Color 5:15 orange.
3. Take the path to the left and color the first clock blue.
4. Color the next clock on the left red.
5. What time does the clock on the right say? _____
6. What time is on the clock at the end of your path? _____

Practical Activities for Practically Everything © 1990 Fearon Teacher Aids

PAPER SPENDING

Cut pictures of food items from the newspaper and label each item with a price less than one dollar. Have each child fold a piece of paper to make three boxes. Each child can choose three food items and glue one in each box. Have children draw the number of pennies, nickels, dimes, and quarters that would be needed to pay for each item beside the picture.

Variation:

Have students total the cost of all three items.

■

TOY BOX

Mount pictures of toys on small pieces of paper. Attach a price tag to each toy. Place all the pictures in a toy box. (Real toys with price tags can be used rather than pictures of toys.) Have each child fold a sheet of paper to make four boxes and choose a toy from the toy box. Have children draw the toy and its price tag in the first box on their papers and draw different varieties of coins that amount to the price on the tag in the other three boxes.

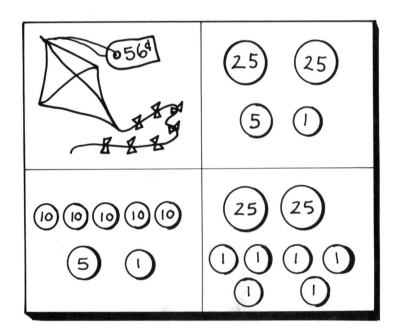

Copy the following format on the chalkboard:

HOW MUCH DID YOU SPEND?

Directions to Children:

You have one dollar to spend. If you could buy any of the items drawn on the chalkboard, which ones would you buy? Remember, you need to spend exactly one dollar. Draw the items on your paper.

Early Birds:

On the back of your paper, write how much money you would need to buy all of the items drawn on the chalkboard.

My Favorite Things

Directions:
Color the pictures of items that you could buy with the amount of money in the box.

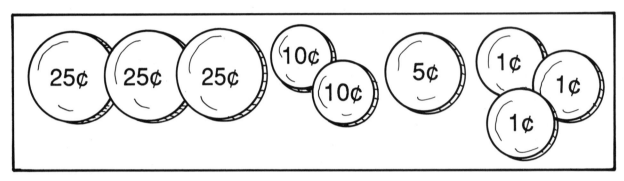

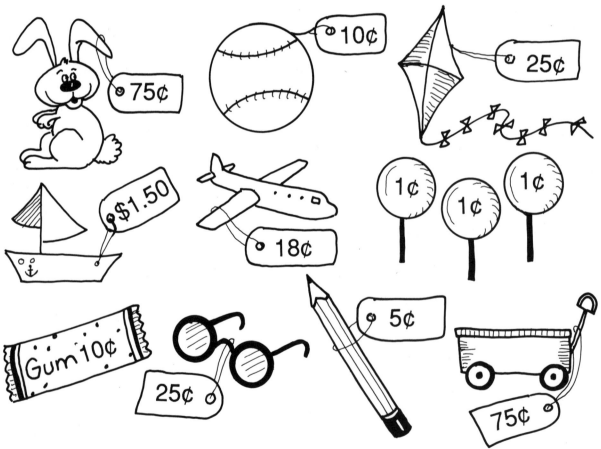

Balloons Galore

Directions:
Find the total price of the two items in each balloon. Color each balloon as follows:

69¢=red   87¢=green   95¢=orange
38¢=blue   77¢=yellow

21¢
56¢

46¢
23¢

73¢
22¢

25¢
13¢

44¢
43¢

IS IT REALLY 1/2?

Discuss with students the concept that objects divided in half have two equal parts. Demonstrate this concept by dividing an apple, paper, shapes, and sets of children in half. Give each student a copy of the worksheet on page 101. Have each child fold a 9" x 12" piece of paper in half lengthwise, unfold the paper, and write "yes" at the top of one column and "no" at the top of the other column. Children cut out the objects and glue them in the "yes" column if they are divided in half and in the "no" column if they are not.

■

PIZZA PARTY

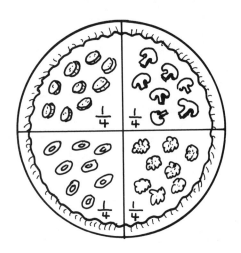

Have each child trace a large circle (provide a pattern) on a piece of paper and draw lines to divide the circle into fourths. Children decorate each fourth of the pizza by drawing different toppings and then label each section "1/4."

■

NAME THAT FRACTION

Give each child a copy of the worksheet on page 102. Have each student fold a 9" x 12" piece of newsprint to make eight boxes. Children can cut out the shaded shapes on the worksheet, glue one in each box on the newsprint, and write the fraction that represents each picture.

Variation:

Cut out the shaded shapes on page 102 and mount them each on a 3" x 5" card. Write the fraction on the back of each card. Students can use the flashcards with a partner to practice recognizing fractional parts.

Name: _____

1/2 or Not?

Practical Activities for Practically Everything © 1990 Fearon Teacher Aids

Name: _____

Shaded Shapes

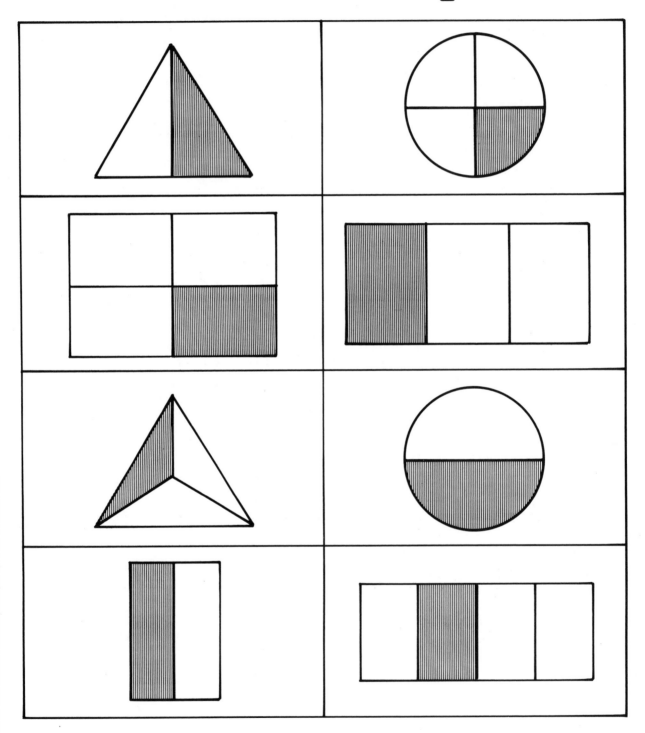

Copy the following list of fractions on the chalkboard:

1/3	1/8
1/2	2/6
1/4	3/8
2/3	5/6

COLORFUL FRACTIONS

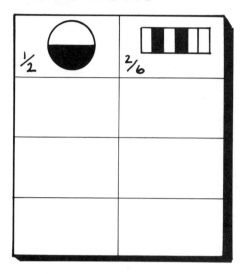

Directions to Children:

Fold your paper to make eight boxes and write a fraction from the list in each box. Draw a shaded picture for each fraction.

Early Birds:

Draw a picture of yourself and two friends on the back of your paper. Color 1/3 of the children.

■

 Provide stamps and stamp pads.

FRACTION FRENZY

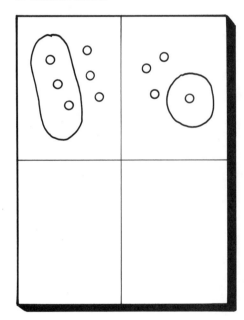

Directions to Children:

1. Fold your paper to make four boxes.
2. Stamp 10 items on your paper in the first box and circle 1/2 of them.
3. Stamp 6 items in the second box and circle 1/3 of them.
4. Stamp 4 items in the third box and circle 1/4 of them.
5. Stamp 8 items in the fourth box and circle 1/2 of them.

Early Birds:

Draw three snakes on the back of your paper. Color one snake 1/2 red. Draw purple dots on 1/3 of another snake. Color orange and black stripes on 1/4 of the last snake.

Cool Treats

Directions:
Look at the pictures below.

How many are divided in half?_____

Color each one red and orange.

How many are divided in thirds?_____

Color each one white, pink, and brown.

How many are divided in fourths?_____

Color each one blue, black, purple, and green.

How many would be hard to divide?_____

Color them brown.

Name:_____

Going Up, Up!

Directions:
1. Color 1/2 of the kites red.
2. Color 1/3 of those that are left blue.
3. Draw orange dots on all the other kites.
4. How many kites have orange dots?_____

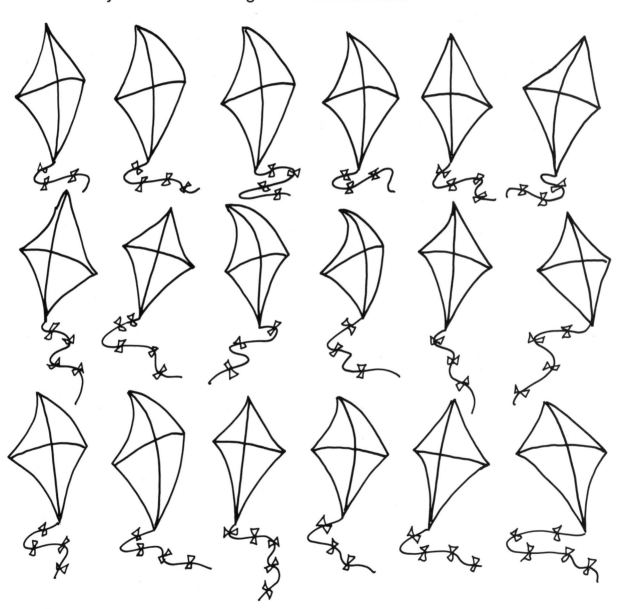

Practical Activities for Practically Everything © 1990 Fearon Teacher Aids

FISHY WORD PROBLEMS

Cut fish shapes from construction paper, number each fish, and then write a word problem on each one. Attach a paper clip to each fish and prepare a fishing pole with a magnet on the end of the fishing line. Each child can catch a fish, write its number on a sheet of paper, and write the answer to the word problem next to it. Children can throw the fish back and catch more.

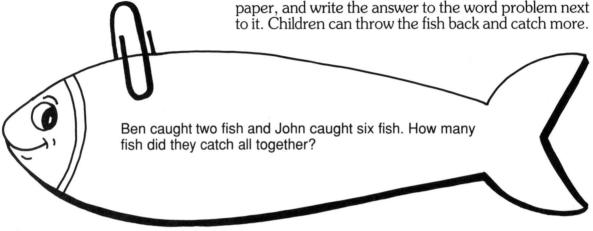

Ben caught two fish and John caught six fish. How many fish did they catch all together?

THE STRAWBERRY PATCH

Give each child a piece of paper cut in the shape of a strawberry to write his or her name and a word problem on. Display all strawberries on a bulletin board entitled "The Strawberry Patch." Later, have each child pick a strawberry off the board, solve the word problem, and write the answer on the back of the strawberry. Return the strawberries to their makers to check for accuracy.

The Strawberry Patch

CHOCOLATE CHIP COOKIES

Write simple word problems on cookie-shaped pieces of paper and place them in a cookie jar. Each child can choose a cookie, solve the problem, and use a circle stamp and stamp pad to illustrate the word problem on a sheet of paper. Have children return the cookies to the jar, so others can use them.

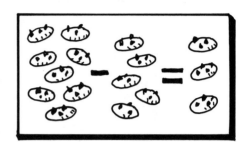

Betty made 8 chocolate chip cookies. Sam ate 3 of them and Bill ate 2. How many were left?

■

THE SWEET SHOP

Write the following word problems on the chalkboard:

1. Mary had 21 pieces of candy. She gave 10 pieces to her friends. How many pieces of candy does she have left?
2. Sam had two dozen doughnuts. Mary gave him another dozen doughnuts. Did he have 24, 36, or 48 doughnuts? Draw your favorite doughnut.
3. Five children were in the ice-cream store, each eating a banana split. Each banana split had two cherries. How many cherries were there?
4. Three children were making a gumdrop tree. They had 11 red, 6 green, 12 orange, and 10 yellow gumdrops. How many gumdrops did they have for the tree?

Directions to Children:

Fold your paper to make four boxes and number the boxes from 1 to 4. Read each word problem. Write one answer in each box on your paper and draw a picture to go with each problem.

Early Birds:

Draw seven of your favorite sweets on the back of your paper.

Rebus Stories

Solve the picture puzzles below.

1. picked  for her mother. Then she

picked  for her mother. How many flowers

did she give her mother?

2. had five  . Two 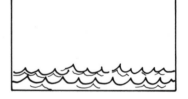 floated out

of sight. How many are left?

3. Eight were in a pen. The farmer wanted 12

 . How many more 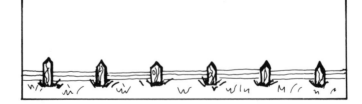 does the farmer

have to buy?

Name: _____

Shaggy Dog

Directions:
Read the story about Bert and draw the number of fleas he still had when he got home.

Bert, the shaggy dog, went for a walk through the tall grass. Seven fleas jumped on Bert. Before he reached the bridge, two fleas jumped off. Bert went for a swim and lost two more fleas. He shook himself off after his swim and rolled on the ground. Here he picked up five more fleas. Bert started to scratch when he got home and three fleas jumped off. How many fleas does Bert have left?

Practical Activities for Practically Everything © 1990 Fearon Teacher Aids

CHUGGING ALONG

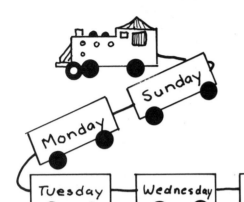

After the class is able to recite the days of the week from memory, begin practicing recognition of the written words. Children can make Days-of-the-Week trains. Write the days of the week on the chalkboard and give each child seven 3" x 5" pieces of colored construction paper on which to copy the days. These pieces will become the train cars. Children can make engines and cabooses from black and red paper. Make a scrap box available to add wheels and details to the trains. Yarn can be used to connect the train cars.

■

FIND THE DAYS

 Give each child a calendar page.

Directions to Children:

1. Use red to circle all the days that are Mondays.
2. Use yellow to color all the days that are Fridays.
3. Draw stars on all the days that are Saturdays.
4. Make a green X on each Wednesday.

Early Birds:

On the back of your paper, write the name of your favorite day of the week. How many of those days are in this month? Write the dates of all of your favorite days.

MY FAVORITE

Give each child a 12" x 18" piece of paper to fold in half. Children can write their favorite day of the week on one half of the paper and their favorite month on the other half. Have children illustrate the words or write a few descriptive sentences on both sides.

MONTH TO MONTH

After practicing the months of the year, give each child construction paper and a pattern to trace twelve circles. Children can write the name of one month on each circle and use felt markers to draw a face on each circle. Scraps can be used to add hats to the circles that signify some holiday or event in each month.

COLD OR WARM?

 Write the following months on the chalkboard:

December
July
February
August
January

Directions to Children:

Copy the months on your paper. Draw mittens beside the name of each month that has cold weather. Draw some bright-colored shorts beside the months that have warm weather.

Early Birds:

Write the names of all the months that you are in school on the back of your paper.

■

MAKE IT SHORT

 Write the days of the week on the board.

Directions to Children:

Copy the names on your paper.
Beside each day, write the short way to write the name (abbreviation).

Early Birds:

On the back of your paper, draw a picture of two things you like to do on Saturday.

Name: _____

Pick Two

Directions:
Read the names of the months of the year. Write the names of two months that go with each picture according to the weather in the area where you live.

January	February	March	April	May	June
July	August	September	October	November	December

_____   _____   _____

_____   _____   _____

_____   _____   _____

_____   _____   _____

Weather Calendar

1. Which day of the week had the most sunny days throughout the month?_____
2. Which day of the week had lightning? _____
3. Which three days did it snow?_____
4. How many Sundays are in this month?_____
5. What are the dates of all the Fridays?_____
6. How many special holidays are in this month? _____
7. How many days were you not supposed to be in school?_____
8. How many days did it rain? _____

January

	Sun.	Mon.	Tues.	Wed.	Thurs.	Fri.	Sat.
		Happy New Year 1	2	3	4	5	6
	7	8	9	10	11	12	13
	14	Martin Luther King 15	16	17	18	19	20
	21	22	23	24	25	26	27
	28	29	30	31			

SAME SHAPE

Write the names of the following shapes on the chalkboard and discuss them: circle, square, triangle, and rectangle. Have each child fold a 12" x 18" piece of newsprint to make four boxes. Children write the name of one shape in each box. Have children look around the room to find objects that match each shape and draw as many as they can in the boxes on their papers.

■

IT'S A CIRCLE!

Have children collect bottle tops, paper towel rolls, paper cups, and other circular items. Put the items into a container and give each child a large piece of paper. Children choose items from the container and trace around them on their papers to create beautiful designs. Or the circular items can be traced onto colored construction paper or wallpaper, cut out, and glued on the large paper.

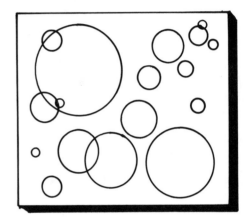

■

RECTANGLE-TRIANGLE DAY

Provide rectangle and triangle patterns of various sizes. Give each child a piece of plain paper and make the scrap box available. Encourage children to create interesting pictures and designs.

SHAPE IT!

 Write the following on the chalkboard:

6 red rectangles
5 blue squares
2 orange circles
8 purple triangles
3 brown rectangles
4 green circles

Directions to Children:

Fold your paper to make six boxes. Copy one set of words into each box and draw the shapes.

Early Birds:

From a magazine, cut out seven pictures that have a square shape. Glue them on the back of your paper.

■

KNOW YOUR SHAPES

 Copy the following words on the chalkboard:

circle
rectangle
triangle
square

Directions to Children:

Fold your paper to make four boxes. Copy one word in each box and draw each shape.

Early Birds:

On the back of your paper, draw five things you eat that have a circular shape. Draw a circle around your favorite.

Name: _____

Plane or Solid

Directions:
Choose from the list of words a name to write under each picture.

circle
triangle
square
rectangle
cone
box
sphere
cube

Practical Activities for Practically Everything © 1990 Fearon Teacher Aids

Make the Pattern

Directions:
Draw the pattern.

_____ _____ _____ _____ _____ _____

  red   blue   red   blue
 circle   triangle   circle   triangle

_____ _____ _____ _____ _____ _____

 yellow   green   red   yellow
rectangle circle   square rectangle

_____ _____ _____ _____ _____ _____

 circle   square rectangle triangle circle

Provide each student with several paper clips. Write the following on the chalkboard:

> student desk
> spelling book
> your foot
> teacher's desk

Directions to Children:

Fold your paper to make four boxes and number the boxes from 1 to 4. Draw one item from the list in each box and write its name underneath. Use your paper clips to measure the length of each item, and record its length next to the picture.

Early Birds:

Use your ruler to measure the length of each item. Write your answers on the back of your paper.

■

This activity should be set up in a learning center area. Empty several boxes of rice into a tub. Place a tablespoon, a one-cup measuring cup, a pint container, and a quart container beside the tub. Write the following questions on cards:

> How many tablespoons of rice are in one cup?
> How many cups of rice make a pint?
> How many pints of rice make a quart?
> How many cups of rice make a quart?

Have the following directions posted at the center for students to read and follow.

Directions:

Fold your paper to make four boxes and number the boxes from 1 to 4. Read each question and find the answer, using the rice and the measuring containers. Write your answers in the boxes.

PAPER CLIP SIZE

RICE PLAY

EGG BASKET

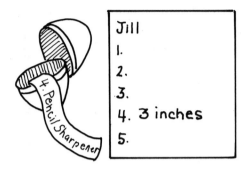

Number small slips of paper and write the name of an object in the room on each one. Put the slips of paper into plastic eggs and put the eggs in a basket. Have each child number an answer sheet with the same amount of numbers as there are eggs in the basket. Children can choose an egg, take out the slip of paper, and measure the object in the room that is listed on the slip. Determine ahead of time whether children will use crayon lengths, paper clip lengths, or a ruler to measure the objects. Have children write their answers next to the corresponding numbers on the answer sheet. Continue until each child has had a chance to measure the item in each egg.

■

THE LONG OR SHORT OF IT

 Write the following questions on the chalkboard:

1. Which is longer, a ruler or a yardstick?
2. Which is greater, a quart of lemonade or a pint of orange juice?
3. Which is shorter, a crayon or a new pencil?
4. Which is smaller, two cups of M & M's or a quart of M & M's?

Directions to Children:

Fold your paper to make four boxes and number the boxes from 1 to 4. Write the answer to each question in the correct box.

Early Birds:

On the back of your paper, draw a picture of two objects that are longer than your foot. Draw a picture of something that holds more water than a bathtub.

Write the following questions on the chalkboard:

How many cups are in a quart?
How many pints are in a quart?
How many cups are in a pint?
How many cups are in a half pint?

CUPS, PINTS, AND QUARTS

Directions to Children:

Fold your paper to make four boxes and number the boxes from 1 to 4. Answer each question by drawing a picture in each box.

Early Birds:

On the back of your paper, draw the number of cups it would take to fill 6 quarts.

■

 Write the following questions on the chalkboard:

How many pieces of candy equal 3 inches?
How many pieces of candy equal 1/2 inch?
How many pieces of candy equal 6 inches?
How many pieces of candy equal 2 inches?
How many pieces of candy equal 1 1/2 inches?

CANDY PIECES

Directions to Children:

Number your paper to 5. If 1 inch = 4 pieces of candy, draw a picture to answer each question.

Early Birds:

On the back of your paper, draw how many pieces of candy it would take to make 15 inches if 1 inch = 3 pieces of candy.

Name: _____

House Study

Directions:
Using a ruler, measure the following objects that are found in your home. Bring your answers back with you to school.

your bed

kitchen table

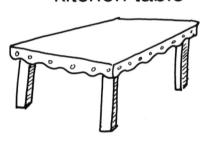

_____

TV

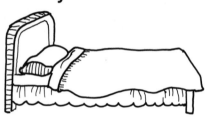

your toothbrush

_____

box of cereal

width of your front door

A Cupful

Directions:
Color all of the objects that could hold more than a quart of water.

pitcher	coffee pot	glass
teacup	swimming pool	bathtub
large pot	birdbath	lake

WHO'S ON FIRST?

Give each child a copy of the ordinal numbers below. Children cut the words apart and glue them in order on another sheet of paper. For extra practice, children write the corresponding number above each word.

first	fifth

sixth	second

seventh	third

fourth	ninth

eighth	tenth

THE SHAPE OF THINGS

ABC **Directions to Children:**

1. Cut out a circle, triangle, rectangle, and square from construction paper.
2. Fold another sheet of paper to make four boxes and number the boxes from 1 to 4.
3. Glue the triangle in the first box.
4. Glue the rectangle in the second box.
5. Glue the circle in the third box.
6. Glue the square in the fourth box.

Early Birds:

On the back of your paper, write six numbers in a row. Put a circle around the first and third numbers. Put an X on the fifth number. Draw a box around the fourth number.

■

KITES, SAILBOATS, AND THINGS

ABC **Directions to Children:**

1. Fold a piece of paper to make four boxes and label the boxes first, second, third, and fourth.
2. In the fourth box, draw a bird.
3. Draw a kite in the third box.
4. Draw a sailboat in the second box and the fourth box.
5. Draw an apple in the third box.
6. Draw a rainbow in the first box and the fourth box.

Early Birds:

On the back of your paper, draw your favorite animal first, your favorite cookie second, your favorite dessert third, and your favorite color fourth.

WHICH IS WHERE?

Give the children each five cards and have them write one of these words on each card: first, second, third, fourth, and fifth. Place some animal pictures on the chalkboard in a horizontal line. Ask the students questions such as "Is the cat first or fifth in line?" Each child can hold up a card to indicate the answer. Continue asking other ordinal number questions about the animals.

■

GO FLY A KITE

 Directions to Children:

1. Draw five kites in a row.
2. Color the third kite blue.
3. Color the fourth kite green.
4. Color the first kite orange.
5. Color the second and fifth kites yellow.

Early Birds:

Design your own paper kite, using materials from the scrap box. Decorate it!

Name: _____

Balloon Day

Directions:
Draw a line from the words to the correct balloons.

twelfth

second

ninth

fifth

eighth

first

third

tenth

fourth

seventh

eleventh

sixth

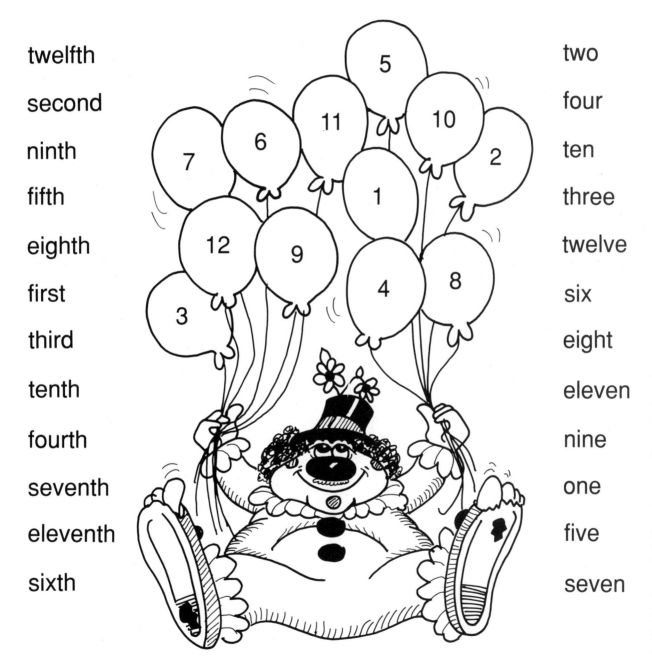

two

four

ten

three

twelve

six

eight

eleven

nine

one

five

seven

Colored Beads

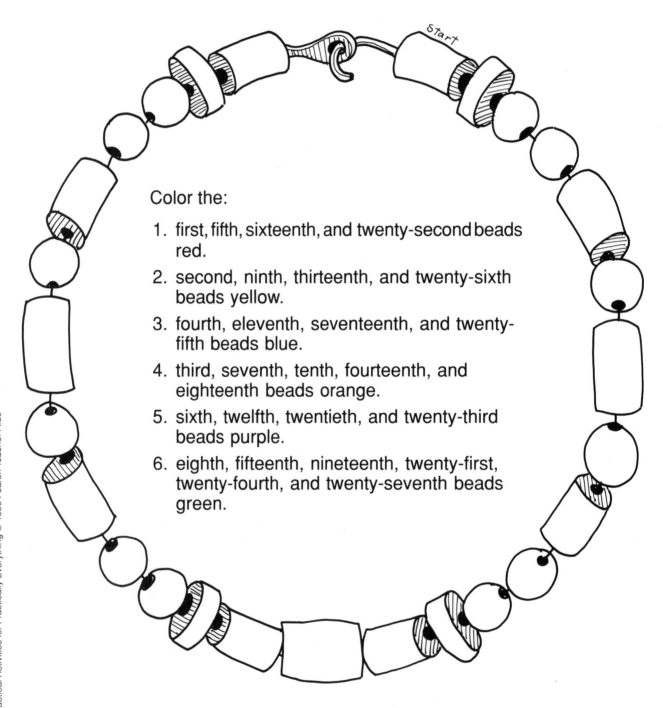

Color the:

1. first, fifth, sixteenth, and twenty-second beads red.

2. second, ninth, thirteenth, and twenty-sixth beads yellow.

3. fourth, eleventh, seventeenth, and twenty-fifth beads blue.

4. third, seventh, tenth, fourteenth, and eighteenth beads orange.

5. sixth, twelfth, twentieth, and twenty-third beads purple.

6. eighth, fifteenth, nineteenth, twenty-first, twenty-fourth, and twenty-seventh beads green.

SPECIAL UNITS

I KNOW MY BUS NUMBER

Give each child a 9" x 12" piece of yellow construction paper and provide a bus pattern. Each child can trace the bus on the paper, cut it out, and write his or her bus number on it. Children can draw windows and people, using felt markers or crayons.

■

ALL SMILES

 Copy the following sentences on the chalkboard:

We work quietly.
We are very loud.
We raise our hands to ask a question.
We never walk in line.

Directions to Children:

Read the sentences and copy them on your paper. If the sentence is a classroom rule, put a smiling face after it. If it is not a classroom rule, put a frowning face after it.

Early Birds:

On the back of your paper, write a new rule for the class.

Have each child fold a 12" x 18" piece of newsprint to make four boxes. Have the children write the name of a teacher or other school personnel (art teacher, librarian, secretary) in each box. Children draw a picture of these people doing their jobs.

FUN TIME

■

 Copy the following sentences on the chalkboard:

1. Lunch costs _____ .
2. Milk is _____ :
3. Dessert will be _____ :
4. Ice cream is _____ :
5. A lunch ticket is _____ :

Also write on the chalkboard the amounts of money that students can choose from to fill in the blanks in each sentence.

LET'S EAT

Directions to Children:

Read the sentences and copy them on your paper. Choose an amount of money from the list to fill in each blank.

Early Birds:

On the back of your paper, draw a picture of your favorite school lunch.

MY PRINCIPAL

Have each child make a picture of the principal after visiting with him or her. Provide construction paper, wallpaper scraps, and yarn for children to use to add interesting details. Children can write a few sentences about the principal at the bottom of their papers. Hang the pictures in the hall for all to see.

■

TAKE ME HOME

 Write the following words on the chalkboard:

scissors
crayons
pencils
box of tissue
glue
school box
eraser
ruler

Directions to Children:

Fold your paper to make eight boxes. Write one word from the list of supplies in each box. Draw a picture for each word. These are supplies you will need.

Early Birds:

On the back of your paper, draw a picture of something you would like to be able to bring to school.

Name: _____

School Rules

Directions:
Cut on the dotted line. Cut the sentences apart. Glue the sentences under the correct pictures.

I sit at the table.	I sit on the swings.
I clean up after lunch.	I take turns jumping.

Practical Activities for Practically Everything © 1990 Fearon Teacher Aids

Name: _____

I Am Older

Directions:
Read each sentence and fill in the blanks with your own answers.

1. Last year I was _____ years old.
   Now I am _____.

2. Last year I was in _____ grade.
   Now I am in _____.

3. My favorite subject last year was _____ .
   This year I like _____ .

4. My teacher last year was _____ .
   This year I have _____ .

5. Last year I couldn't _____ .
   This year I can _____ .

6. Last year I didn't like _____ .
   This year I could do without _____ .

7. My best friend last year was _____ .
   This year my best friend is _____ .

8. This year I wish we could learn more about _____ .

MACARONI NECKLACES

Cut a necklace length of yarn for each child. Dip the yarn ends in glue and allow them to dry. The glue will stiffen the yarn ends and make threading the macaroni easier. Provide various shapes of macaroni for children to thread onto their strings to make necklaces. Encourage students to make a pattern by mixing the shapes (two short pieces, one long piece, two short pieces, and so on).

Variation:

You may also want to dye some of the macaroni so that children can make color patterns as well as shape patterns.

■

TURKEY HANDS

Have each child trace his or her hand on a piece of paper and decorate the print to look like a turkey. On each feather (finger), children can write one thing they are thankful for.

ONE, TWO, THREE, FOUR

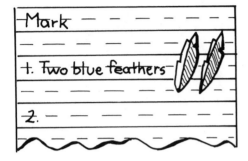

 Write the following phrases on the chalkboard:

two blue feathers
three yellow teepees
five brown turkeys
one orange pumpkin
four black Pilgrim hats

Directions to Children:

Copy each set of words on your paper. Draw a picture to show the meaning of each set of words.

Early Birds:

On the back of your paper, write as many Thanksgiving words as you can think of.

■

LET'S GIVE THANKS

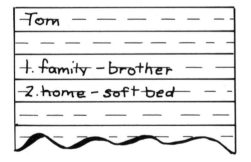

 Write the following list of words on the chalkboard:

family
friends
home
school
country

Directions to Children:

Copy the list of words onto your paper, writing one word on each line. Beside each word, write something you are thankful for that fits that category.

Early Birds:

On the back of your paper, make a list of foods you would like to eat for Thanksgiving dinner.

Give each child a copy of the sentences below and two 8 1/2" x 11" sheets of plain paper. Have children place the two sheets of paper on top of each other and fold them in half to make a booklet. Staple the booklet along the fold line and have children cut the sentence strips apart. Children can write the title "Pilgrims and Indians" on the booklet cover and then glue one sentence strip in the correct order at the bottom of each page. Children can illustrate the sentences to complete the booklet.

PILGRIMS AND INDIANS

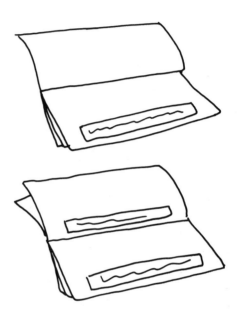

| The Indians and the Pilgrims ate together. |
| The Pilgrims came to a new land in the Mayflower. |
| The Indians brought food to the Thanksgiving feast. |
| The Indians taught the Pilgrims how to plant corn. |
| The Pilgrims were hungry their first winter. |

Name: _____

Food, Shelter, and Clothing

Directions:
Cut on the dotted line. Cut the pictures apart. Glue each picture under the correct heading.

Food	Shelter	Clothing

- ✄

Name: _____

Turkey in the Barnyard

1. Draw 2 brown turkeys on the fence.
2. Draw a red barn.
3. Draw 3 orange pumpkins in the field.
4. Draw 10 red apples on the tree.
5. Make the fence yellow.
6. Draw 2 Pilgrim children.
7. Draw 3 Indians.
8. Draw some corn growing in the field.

FASHION SHOW

After discussing winter weather in various parts of the United States, give each child a popsicle stick and a copy of the paper doll. Each child can cut out the doll, glue it on the popsicle stick, and dress it according to the weather conditions in the chosen area (Hawaii, Alaska, Florida, and so on). Provide construction paper, wallpaper books, and cloth scraps for children to use as they dress their dolls.

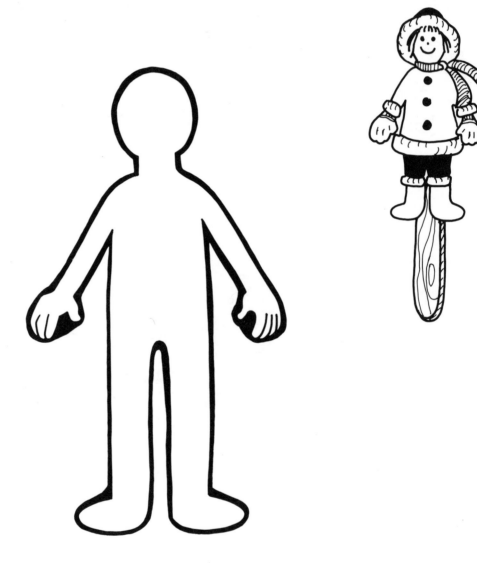

Provide each child with a blank calendar page to record the temperature and weather conditions for every day of the month. Decide as a class what time each day you will check and record the data. Set a class standard for weather symbols. On the back of the calendar pages, provide graph lines so that after the data has been recorded for the entire month, graphs can be made to form some conclusions.

FEBRUARY

Sun.	Mon.	Tues.	Wed.	Thurs.	Fri.	Sat.
		1 * * * 30°	2 32°	3 45°	4 40°	5 * * * 33°
6 25°	7 37°	8 41°				

∎

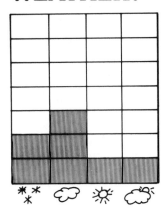

WHAT'S THE WEATHER?

0-20 21-30 31-40 41-50 51-60

WINTER WORDS

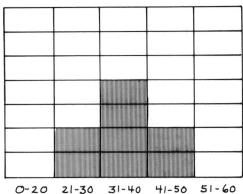 Write the following list of words on the chalkboard:

hot cocoa	bells	Rudolph
sled	skiing	gifts
Christmas trees	valentines	mittens
snow		

Directions to Children:

Number your paper to 10. Read the winter words and then write them in ABC order on your paper.

Early Birds:

On the back of your paper, draw a picture of the holiday that comes on March 17. Did you use a lot of green?

FUN IN WINTER

Discuss winter activities with children, such as sledding, drinking hot chocolate, building fires in the fireplace, and skiing. Make a list of these activities on the chalkboard. Have each child fold a 12" x 18" piece of paper to make four boxes and choose a winter activity from the list to write in each box. Make available some interesting materials for students to use to construct 3-D pictures to illustrate their choices.

Material suggestions:

small sticks	wallpaper books
toothpicks	scraps of cloth
cotton balls	foil (silver and colored)
construction paper	colored tissue
felt markers	cotton swabs and
colored cellophane	white tempera paint

■

WINTER HOLIDAYS

 Copy the following list of winter holidays and dates on the chalkboard:

New Year's Day	January 1
Christmas	December 25
Martin Luther King's birthday	January 15
George Washington's birthday	February 22
Abraham Lincoln's birthday	February 12
Valentine's Day	February 14
Ground Hog's Day	February 2
classmates' birthdays	

Directions to Children:

Fold your paper to make four boxes. Write one winter holiday and its date in each box and draw a picture of each.

Early Birds:

On the back of your paper, draw a picture of your favorite holiday. Be sure to draw yourself in the picture, too!

Variation:

Write the dates in a separate list so that children can practice matching the correct date with the holiday.

Name: _____

Let's Travel

Directions:
Color all the things you could use to get around better in the snow.

Practical Activities for Practically Everything © 1990 Fearon Teacher Aids

Mr. Snowman

Directions:
Follow the directions to complete the snowman. Write as many words as you can think of that have to do with snow around the snowman.

1. Draw a black hat.
2. Draw a carrot nose.
3. Draw two charcoal eyes.
4. Draw four square buttons on the snowman's middle section.
5. Draw two stick arms.
6. Draw a red and blue striped scarf around his neck.
7. Draw two green boots.
8. Draw three feathers in his hat.
9. Draw a mouth so that the snowman can talk to you!

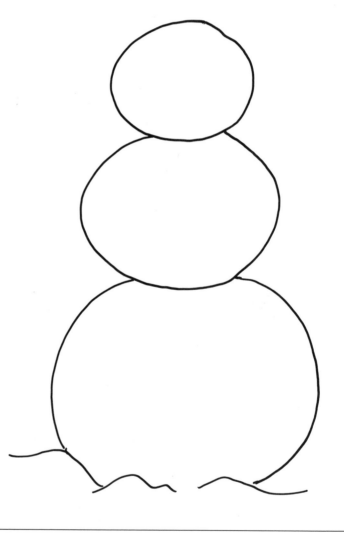

Have each child draw eyes, nose, ears, or a mouth on a sheet of plain paper. Children can color, cut out, and glue the part they drew on the top half of a sheet of lined paper. After a discussion of good health and hygiene habits, have students write some ways to care for the part they drew.

BODY WORKS

■

Because primary children are very susceptible to chicken pox, colds, and other viruses, they are often absent from school for a few days at a time. During your health unit, have children design some "Get Well" cards with cheerful messages. Provide a variety of materials. Stress neatness and correct spelling. Keep these cards in a special box and choose one to send to an ill class member when needed.

GET WELL QUICK

■

Discuss ways children can help prevent the spreading of a cold and list the ideas on the chalkboard. Have each child draw what they think a "cold bug" might look like on a sheet of plain paper. Children can choose an idea from the chalkboard to copy on the bottom of their pages. Display a magnified picture of an actual cold virus.

THE COLD BUG

HEALTHY NEWS

Explain to children that a rebus story is one with words and pictures. Give each child a magazine to look for pictures and create a classroom rebus story on the chalkboard together. Once students have the idea, ask them to create their own imaginary stories about a time they were sick and couldn't go out to play or a time they visited the doctor. Using pictures will encourage children to include words that they would ordinarily avoid because they cannot spell them. Repeat this activity throughout the year and you will notice the children becoming real budding authors!

One ☀ day, a 🧍 rode my 🚲

and had an

■

FAST FOOD

Meat	Bread	Milk
bacon	cereal	cheese
		yogurt

ᴬᴮ꜀ Copy the following list of food words on the chalkboard:

ham	cheese
cereal	nuts
fish	muffins
ice cream	bacon
biscuits	bagels
steak	cottage cheese
yogurt	

Directions to Children:

Fold your paper to make three boxes. Label the top of the columns with the words "meat," "bread," and "milk." Copy the food words on your paper in the correct column.

Early Birds:

Glue magazine pictures of your favorite fruits and vegetables on the back of your paper.

Have children think about foods they would choose to make a really terrific breakfast. The children cut out from newspapers pictures and prices for each breakfast item and glue them on a sheet of plain paper. If they can't find what they are looking for in the newspapers, the children can draw the pictures. The children should also include the total cost of the breakfast items.

FOOD FOR THOUGHT

Variation:

Have children choose food for lunch or dinner.

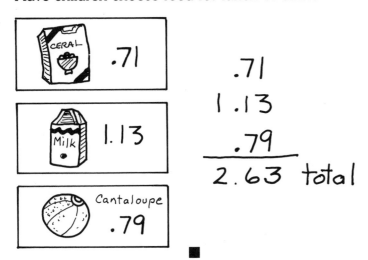

```
 .71
1.13
 .79
-----
2.63  total
```

ORDER ME

ABC Write the following list of body parts on the chalkboard:

leg	wrist
toe	chin
neck	arm
finger	head
elbow	nose
knee	foot

Directions to Children:

Number your paper to 12. Copy the body part words on your paper in ABC order.

Early Birds:

Write a story in which two body parts are talking to each other.

HEALTH **147**

Funny Parts

Directions:
Write the funny parts on the correct lines.

| funny bone | shin | big toe |
| belly button | pinkie | blinkers |

Sweet Dreams

Directions:
Draw a dream in the bubble that you might have if you had eaten a whole pepperoni pizza before you went to bed.

LET'S GROW A BEAN PLANT

Give each child a paper cup and a bean. Provide potting soil and ask each child to plant the bean in the paper cup. Children can observe the plants and record the growth on a chart.

Variation:

Children can observe the bean sprout if it is first placed between wet paper towels in the paper cup. Then the sprouted bean can be transferred to soil.

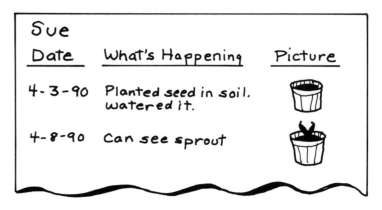

■

IN YOUR EASTER BONNET

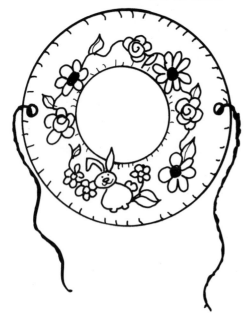

Give each child a paper plate with yarn attached on both sides. Brainstorm with the children to recall celebrations and traditions associated with Easter and spring, and then provide a variety of materials for children to use to decorate the plates to look like Easter bonnets. When the children have finished making the hats, they can tie the yarn under their chins to hold the hats on their heads. Plan to have an Easter parade or vote on the most unusual or original hats.

Have each child cut out a flower picture from a magazine, glue it on a sheet of paper, and write a description of the flower below the picture. Put all the pages together to make a class flower booklet. Add a cover and a title page.

FLOWER PARADE

Variation:

Try the same idea with bird pictures.

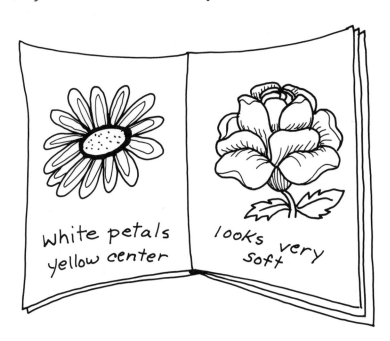

BEAUTIFUL BUTTERFLIES

 After discussing the stages of a butterfly's life, write the following words on the chalkboard:

egg
caterpillar
pupa
butterfly

Directions to Children:

Fold your paper to make four boxes. Copy one word in each box and draw a picture of each stage of a butterfly's life.

Early Birds:

Use a library book to find two different kinds of butterflies. Draw and label them on the back of your paper.

Name: _____

Babies Galore

Directions:
Cut on the dotted line. Cut the baby animal names apart. Glue each baby animal name next to its mother's name.

1. horse	
2. cat	
3. dog	
4. sheep	
5. cow	
6. duck	
7. hen	
8. bear	

✂ -

lamb	cub
duckling	puppy
kitten	colt
chick	calf

Practical Activities for Practically Everything © 1990 Fearon Teacher Aids

Name: _____

Food, Flowers, and Other Plants

Directions:
Cut on the dotted line. Cut the pictures apart and glue them under the correct heading.

Flowers	Foods	Other Plants

154 SPRING

ABC ANIMALS

 Write the following list of wild animals on the chalkboard:

antelope	lion
elephant	monkey
giraffe	panda
hippopotamus	tiger
kangaroo	zebra

Directions to Children:

Number your paper to 10. Write the animal names in ABC order on your paper.

Early Birds:

On the back of your paper, draw a picture of your favorite wild animal.

■

SHAPE AND WRITE

Have each child fold a piece of paper into fourths and cut the paper apart on the fold lines to make four pages for an animal booklet. Give each child a copy of the wild animal pictures on page 156. Children can choose four animals from the page, cut them out, and glue one on each of their booklet pages. Have children write a descriptive sentence about each animal, staple the pages together, and decorate their booklet covers.

An elephant has big ears.

■

PICK A WILD ONE

Find pictures of wild animals in magazines or make several copies of the pictures on page 156. Put the pictures in a paper bag. Each child can choose an animal from the bag, glue it onto a 12" x 18" sheet of paper, and then draw the animal's habitat around it.

Animals in the Wild

After a discussion of animal habitats, copy the following words on the chalkboard:

Arctic
Desert
Jungle
Ocean

Directions to Children:

Fold your paper into four boxes and write one word from the list in each box. Draw as many animals as you can think of that live in each area.

Early Birds:

Find a picture in a magazine of one of these wild animals and glue it on the back of your paper.

■

 Write the following list of animals on the chalkboard:

leopard
cow
bear
horse
seal
dog
camel
cat
cheetah
gorilla

Directions to Children:

Number your paper to 10. Copy the name of each animal on your paper and then write "yes" beside each wild animal and "no" beside each animal that is not wild.

Early Birds:

On the back of your paper, write the names of two other wild animals.

ANIMALS AT HOME

ARE THEY WILD?

Loud or Quiet?

Directions:
Read the list of animals at the bottom of the page. Write the names of the animals that make loud sounds under the lion column. Write the names of the animals that make quiet sounds under the cat column.

Loud

Quiet

1. _____   1. _____

2. _____   2. _____

3. _____   3. _____

4. _____   4. _____

5. _____   5. _____

tiger   elephant   bobcat
rabbit   antelope   gorilla
snake   deer   chipmunk
                             leopard

Name: _____

A Really Wild Animal

Directions:
Follow each step to make a really wild animal!

1. Draw a large body.
2. Draw a small head.
3. Draw three floppy ears.
4. Draw four skinny legs.
5. Draw a short tail.
6. Put stripes on the legs.
7. Put spots on the body.
8. Draw feet and add long toenails.
9. Draw a nose with a bump on it.
10. Draw a large mouth and small beady eyes.

Practical Activities for Practically Everything © 1990 Fearon Teacher Aids